D1159924

SAM
THE HIGHEST JUMPER OF THEM ALL

SAM
THE HIGHEST JUMPER
OF THEM ALL
OR
THE LONDON COMEDY

William Saroyan

FABER AND FABER

24 Russell Square

London

First published in mcmlxi
by Faber and Faber Limited
24 Russell Square London W.C.1
Printed in Great Britain by
Latimer Trend & Co Ltd Plymouth

Inquiries concerning professional performing rights should be addressed to William Saroyan, care of Faber and Faber Ltd., 24 Russell Square, London, W.C.1.

Inquiries concerning amateur performing rights should be addressed to Samuel French Ltd., 26 Southampton Street, London, W.C.2.

This play is dedicated to
everybody associated with the Theatre Royal,
with thanks.

Sam the Highest Jumper of Them All, or *The London Comedy* was made-up, written, and directed on the stage of the Theatre Royal, Angel Lane, Stratford, London. Two benefit performances were given on the 4th and 5th of April 1960, and the play opened on April 6th. The settings were designed by John Bury, costumes by David Walker, dances by Jean Newlove, songs by the playwright. The cast was as follows:

SAM HARK-HARKALARK, BANK CLERK	*Murray Melvin*
TED OWLETT, BANK CLERK	*Griffith Davies*
MR. HORNIMAN, PRESIDENT OF THE BANK	*Robert Henderson*
POOR MAN, AND PSYCHIATRIST	*Robin Chapman*
MISS GALWAY, AND SOCIAL WORKER	*Jean Conroy*
ANN MOON	*Claire Isbister*
GYPSY, AND SAM'S GRANDMOTHER	*Rosemary Johnson*
RACING TIPSTER, BOBBY, EXECUTED MAN, AND WORKER	*Anthony Booth*
WALLY WAILER, GUITAR-PLAYER, SINGER	*Frank Coda*
BLIND MAN, MAN WITH CLOCK, AND DISCUSSER OF GUN AND EGG-BEATER	*Michael Forrest*
DAISY DIMPLE, ACTRESS	*Jan Arnold*
FATHER FINNEGAN, AND SAM'S GRANDFATHER	*William Sherwood*
INSPECTOR OVERBOARD, SCOTLAND YARD	*John Maitland*
CAPTAIN DATCHIKVILI, U.S.S.R.	*Ori Levy*
AMBASSADOR FROM THE AUDIENCE TO THE PLAY	*Robert Mill*

The play is set in Stratford, London: a square playing area upon which a portion of the London Underground Map is painted in bright colours.

Introduction

ACT ONE

At the Bank

ACT TWO

At Sam's Home and at the Bank

The Songs:

The Ballad of Nellie Miller, or We Were only Having Fun

Too Many People

Around the Moon

Sam The Highest Jumper of Them All

INTRODUCTION

In order to talk about this play I must briefly review my work in the theatre.

Late in 1938 I made a one-act play of a short story called *The Man With the Heart in the Highlands*, written late in 1935, after I had returned to San Francisco from my first visit to Europe, and to Soviet Armenia and Russia.

Early in 1939 I enlarged the work, although it remained a one-act play. It was produced in New York in the spring of that year, under the new title of *My Heart's in the Highlands*. Although the playing time was only an hour, it was presented as a full-length play, and nobody complained on that account.

Most of the critics, however, complained on other accounts: the play was surely a joke, the playwright was surely pulling the leg of the public, the play was not a play, the play followed no known rules, the play had no form, no meaning, no purpose, the play was sentimental, stupid, childish, and an insult to civilized men and women.

Well, of course, a writer really never knows about such things, and he must be told by those who do.

In May of 1939 I wrote another play and it opened in October: *The Time of Your Life*. It won two prizes. There were only two in the U.S. at that time, perhaps there are now twenty-two.

A third play, *Love's Old Sweet Song*, was produced in 1940. The producers with whom I had worked were so eager for box-office success and nothing else that I decided to found my own theatre and to produce my own plays, with my own money. The first production was *The Beautiful People*, the second was *Across the Board on Tomorrow Morning*. The first did fairly well, but the second flopped, and the theatre I had founded was finished.

I had had five plays on Broadway. The sixth, which appeared late in 1943, was *Get Away Old Man*. It closed after seven performances.

In 1947 I began to write plays again, but didn't offer them to producers.

In 1957 I allowed *The Cave Dwellers* to be produced. The same old charges were made by the same old critics.

That sums up my produced work in the U.S. theatre, and brings me to *Sam the Highest Jumper of Them All*.

From Paris in February of 1960 I wrote to Joan Littlewood to say that I had enjoyed seeing Brendan Behan's play *The Hostage* in London. The manager of the Theatre Royal, Gerald Raffles, replied and invited me to direct one of my own plays at the Theatre Royal. I sent him three published plays and two ideas I had for new plays. He chose one of the three plays, *Jim Dandy*, but a few days later he wondered if I might be able to make a play in the theatre out of one of the ideas. I said I could, although the procedure would make great demands on the players. On March 1st I arrived in London and went to work, meeting players and writing the play. A rough draft was finished in nine or ten days. Two benefit performances were given early in April, and on the 6th the play opened to the press and general public. The house was packed and the response of the audience gave me the impression that they liked it. The reviews, however, informed me that the play was meaningless and amateurish.

I replied to the critics, in part, as follows:

> *The Savoy Hotel*
> *London*
> *10th April, 1960*

A Letter to Fifteen Drama Critics

Miss Elizabeth Frank, the *News Chronicle*
Mr. Robert Muller, the *Daily Mail*
Mr. Bernard Levin, the *Daily Express*
The Drama Critic of *The Times*
Mr. Dick Richards, the *Daily Mirror*
Mr. W. A. Darlington, the *Daily Telegraph*
Mr. T. C. Worsley, *The Financial Times*
Mr. Philip Hope-Wallace, the *Manchester Guardian*
Mr. Felix Barker, the *Evening News*
Mr. Robert Wraight, the *Star*

Mr. Milton Shulman, the *Evening Standard*
The Drama Critic of the *Daily Herald*
Mr. Jack Lewis, *Reynolds' News*
Mr. J. W. Lambert, the *Sunday Times*
Mr. Irving Wardle, the *Observer*

Dear Miss Frank:
and Gentlemen:

I have read with a great deal of interest your reviews of *Sam the Highest Jumper of Them All*, or *The London Comedy*.

I hope you won't mind if I comment on this work in a single letter rather than in fifteen separate ones.

I have never had a play that has won all of the drama critics of New York, but this is the first time that one of my plays has failed to win at least one or two of the critics. As there are fifteen of you, I am obliged to give this fact the importance it obviously demands.

Easiest of all would be for me to agree that the play is bad, or at any rate that it doesn't work, but that's a little too easy, and hardly honest or useful.

Fifteen years ago the Hiroshima and Nagasaki bombs gave the dramatists of the world clear instructions, which as far as I know have not been heeded.

The basis of drama continues to be emotionality, even though the new reality has made emotionality obsolete. Now, nothing in the world can make even the most righteous emotionality anything more or better than simple foolishness, because if you carry this emotionality through to its inevitable conclusion you have *got* to use the new power, and you'd better not. Hence, you'd better not be emotional either.

The grand tradition of raging against "fate, or something just as bad", won't do any more. You may reason but you may not rage.

Now, if art is to have any relation to reality—and I know of no other excuse for it—it has got to make drama (form, meaning, beauty, truth) out of intelligence, humour, wit, humility and self-criticism. If there is an enemy, he must be identified as one's self. It is useless to call the other fellow the enemy, while you carry on precisely as he does.

Whether used destructively or constructively, the new power is

13

giving us a new identity. Some of us are aware of this and some of us aren't. When the identity of the whole race changes, reality changes, and more slowly, art.

The use of force, even as a threat, is out. If it isn't, we may have to believe that, deliberately or unconsciously, we rejoice in the possibility of self-destruction.

All of this is in the play in the form of kindergarten drama and fun. The staging is in a straight line. There is no razzle-dazzle, no tom-tom beat, no running, ranting, raving, or other hamming-up. If man is always potentially a fraud, this is quite clear.

Plays are for people, however. Drama critics are also people, and so you have a perfect right to protest that first and foremost, as they say, a play has got to be something effective in acceptable terms on the boards of a theatre.

Since the play, for you, wasn't, you have me there.

It was, and is, however, for me. I also am people, so where do we go from here? I write plays and you write criticism. There are fifteen of you and one of me.

I say Sam is a good play. I am sorry you say it isn't. One of us is obviously mistaken. Knowing the paltry little I know, I cannot believe it is me.

WILLIAM SAROYAN

The play ran for four weeks. I do not believe it is my fault that the critics didn't understand it. The play is quite simple: it is contemptuous of the phoney, that's all, even when the phoney appears to be the gospel. There are no hidden meanings in it.

Paris, June 1960

Act One

SAM HARK-HARKALARK *walks on stage and stands behind his counter. Then,* EDWARD OWLETT *enters and takes his place at his counter.* MR. HORNIMAN *enters with two bags of money, one for* SAM *and one for* TED, *then leans upon a pedestal.*

SAM: (*to audience*). How do you do? I am Sam. This is a play, pure and simple, and in the play this is a bank somewhere in Stratford, not far from this theatre.

The distinguished-looking gentleman is the President of the bank, Mr. Telford Horniman, who came over from America forty-five years ago. The seedy-looking young man is Edward Owlett, or Ted, who has been with the bank six years.

All of us are imagined of course, for the purpose of the structure, style, form and meaning of the play, if any.

We all know that nothing here is real as we know reality outside this theatre, in the street, in the remainder of London, and in the world itself, and so we shall not try to be real in that way, since total success would make it necessary for us to leave the theatre immediately, and I don't believe we want to do that.

Two hours more or less, including the intermission, is what's at stake, plus the price of admission. For which we hope to provide you with a little amusement.

This is the cue for a bell to ring indicating that the bank is open. Now, it doesn't matter that bells do not ring before banks are opened. Nothing of that sort matters in this play, if in fact it matters anywhere else. (HORNIMAN *rings a school-bell.*)

15

There it is. We have used up a little time during
which to become settled, and perhaps to expect the
worst. We begin, then. Sam the Highest Jumper of
Them All, or The London Comedy. (*Suddenly.*)
Action. Lights. Madness. (*He smiles.*) Perhaps you
won't mind awfully. Thank you.

(SAM *returns to his place. A man comes to Ted's
window.*)

MAN: I'd like to borrow a little money.

TED: Yes, sir, how much?

MAN: Well, I need a hundred pounds.

TED: What security do you have? A house? A car?
Furniture?

MAN: (*Shakes his head.*)

TED: Anything at all?

MAN: I've got three small children.

TED: The bank won't lend you any money on three small
children.

MAN: Two boys and a girl. (*He shows snapshot.*) Here's a
picture of them. Dan. John. And Rose.

TED: Dan, John, and Rose. They're nice-looking kids.
Better try to borrow from a friend.

MAN: *They* need money, too. Could I borrow, then, *fifty*
pounds?

TED: Without security the bank wouldn't let you have
one pound.

MAN: Why not? What's a bank for?

HORNIMAN: Yes, yes, what seems to be the trouble, Mr. Owlett?

TED: This man needs one hundred pounds, sir, but he
hasn't got any security. Only three small children.
Dan, John, and Rose.

HORNIMAN: (*to* MAN). Dan, John, and Rose don't count, my dear
man. The bank will be only too happy to lend you
at six per cent interest any amount you care to
name if you will be good enough to come to the
bank only when you are able to abide by the rules.
If you are to borrow £10,000, for instance, you
must have something tangible and real that is worth

16

at least £30,000.

MAN: I've got a good job. It's just that it doesn't pay as much as I need. Couldn't you make an exception?

HORNIMAN: Impossible, sir. If everybody who needed money expected a loan without security the banks would fail in a year.

MAN: Why?

HORNIMAN: Because people don't pay their debts unless they have to.

MAN: I'll pay my debt.

HORNIMAN: You may very well *intend* to do so, but in the meantime you may also die, and then where would the bank be?

MAN: I don't expect to die, but if I did, where would my kids be? Aren't kids worth something?

HORNIMAN: Not to the bank. I'm afraid there is no point to any further discussion, Mr. Owlett. (*He goes back to his pedestal.* TED *hands back the snapshot. The* MAN *stands perplexed and angry, looking around the bank, then goes.* MISS GALWAY *steps up to* SAM'S *window.* SAM *opens the book and reads her name.*)

SAM: You wish to make a deposit, Miss Galway?

GALWAY: No thank you. I'd like to make a withdrawal, if I may.

SAM: In that case you will have to write out a cheque.

GALWAY: I'd very much like to take out all of it, if I may.

SAM: One pound, six and two? You wish to *close* your account, Miss Galway?

GALWAY: Yes. I'm going to have a baby.

SAM: Oh? I'm afraid there's a closing charge of tuppence, Miss Galway. Couldn't you manage on six shillings and tuppence and leave the pound?

GALWAY: I'm afraid not. Having a baby is rather expensive. (*Pause.*) *Not* having a baby is rather expensive, *too*.

SAM: Very well, Miss Galway. We're certainly sorry to lose your account.

GALWAY: Oh, I'm sorry to *have* it lost.

SAM: Has our service been satisfactory?

B

GALWAY: Oh, yes. You've always treated me with a great deal of kindness here at this bank.

SAM: Then we may expect the opening of a new account when fortune favours?

GALWAY: Yes, I think so. If fortune ever does.

SAM: I'm sure it will some day. An inheritance perhaps.

GALWAY: An inheritance would be most welcome. I'd certainly like things to be a little nicer for my daughter or son than they have been for me. Having things nicer is rather expensive too, isn't it?

SAM: Yes, I'm afraid it is.

GALWAY: Even just *a little* nicer.

SAM: (*Stamps the book, initials it, counts the money.*) One pound six shillings. The account is closed, then.

GALWAY: Thank you ever so much.

SAM: Goodbye, Miss Galway.

GALWAY: Goodbye, Mister . . . ?

SAM: Hark-Harkalark. Sam Hark-Harkalark.

GALWAY: Goodbye, Mr. Hark-Harkalark. If it's a boy, perhaps you won't mind if I give him *your* name.

SAM: Sam?

GALWAY: No, your other name.

SAM: Oh, you couldn't do that. Your husband wouldn't like it.

GALWAY: (*Quickly*) Really? Do you know him? Have you seen him? Woolworth Rockefeller Ford? He's an American soldier.

SAM: Oh, I *know* he is, but I'm afraid I *haven't* seen him. (*She takes her place behind another girl at* FATHER FINNEGAN's *table.*)

FINNEGAN: Nothing today, Coral, my dear.

CORAL: Nothing at all? Not even sixpence like yesterday?

FINNEGAN: The pension money will come again day after tomorrow, however. (CORAL *goes.*) Nothing, Pearl, my dear.

GALWAY: I don't know what to do. Shall I have it stopped?

FINNEGAN: Oh no, that would be murder.

GALWAY: I don't *want* to. It's just that without a father to

18

help me bring up my baby, I thought it might be better for my baby not to be born. Sometimes I almost wish *I* hadn't been born. I *won't* go where I'm expected to go. I'm too ashamed.

FINNEGAN: I will help you, somehow. Whenever there is nowhere else to go please come here.

GALWAY: This afternoon?

FINNEGAN: Yes, this afternoon.

GALWAY: (*Softly*) Thank you.

(*She goes.* FATHER FINNEGAN *picks up a Qantas satchel and goes.* ANN MOON *enters and goes straight to* SAM'S *window.*)

ANN: I'd like to take out all of my money, please.

SAM: Are you going to have a baby, too?

ANN: Is that a condition of closing the account?

SAM: Oh no. I just thought perhaps you might have met an American, too.

ANN: I want my money because I need it.

SAM: (*Reads from her bank book.*) Ann Moon. One pound eight and four, minus a closing charge of tuppence.

ANN: But I need the *full* amount—for new shoes.

SAM: I'll pay the tuppence out of my pocket.

ANN: Oh no, I don't want you to do *that*.

SAM: It's all right. You see, this is my first day as a full-fledged clerk, after almost a year as office boy, and I won't miss the tuppence at all.

ANN: Are you sure?

SAM: Quite. And I'm glad you're not going to have a baby. I mean, if you didn't want to have one, on account of the population explosion. It's not actually an explosion of course, but I've heard they're asking women to think twice about it.

ANN: I don't have to think about it at all. (*Pause*) I'm glad you've been promoted.

SAM: I've worked awfully hard for it.

ANN: And this is your first day?

SAM: Yes, and you're my second transaction. I know I'm

19

being watched. Behind me, that's Mr. Horniman himself, the President of the bank. (*Pause*) He started here forty-five years ago.

ANN: Forty-five years is a long time.

SAM: Not at all. It only *seems* long afterwards. In any case, I'm going to do exactly what he did.

ANN: Doesn't he mind if you chat this way?

SAM: Oh no, that's precisely what he wants me to do. This is a family bank, he says. Everybody who comes here is a member of our family. This bank is made of flesh and blood. It is not a machine. And we're not in a hurry the way some of the other banks are. There is always time to be courteous and considerate, he says.

(HORNIMAN *goes.*)

ANN: He's going now.

SAM: Oh, I know he's going.

ANN: *How* do you know?

SAM: Some kind of eau-de-Cologne he uses every half-hour. He can be very kind, but he doesn't like any liberties to be taken. When you speak to him you've got to be awfully respectful. Only the people who have been here thirty years are permitted to address him as Mr. Horniman, and most of *them* don't do it. They say sir, too.

ANN: Do you really want to stay thirty years just to be able to say Mr. Horniman?

SAM: Forty if need be.

ANN: Does it mean all that to you?

SAM: To be President of the bank? What else is there worth being?

ANN: There must be *something* else. I'd hate to imagine what you might believe would be worth being had you gone to work a year ago for an undertaker.

SAM: Oh, no, I've always been a banker.

ANN: I wouldn't work in a bank for anything in the world.

SAM: Why not?

20

ANN: Why, the danger of it, for one thing. The robbers.

SAM: We have ways to deal with *them*. This button right here—just barely touch it and the alarm sounds, and it's very loud.

ANN: Do you mean *noise* can stop a bullet? You could be standing there, alive one minute, and dead the next. And then where would your great career be? Where would *you* be? And not only that. You might endanger the lives of everybody else in the bank.

SAM: Well, I certainly wouldn't want to endanger the lives of others. I'd feel most unhappy if somebody *else* got killed, too.

ANN: You wouldn't mind so much if it was only yourself?

SAM: No, of course not. My duty is to defend the money.

ANN: Do you really believe money is more important than life?

SAM: Ah, well, I can see you don't understand banking.

ANN: I believe you want to be a hero of some kind.

SAM: If I had no choice, I wouldn't mind. It would mean immediate promotion, you know.

ANN: What a silly word.

SAM: (*Smiles, stamps the book, and initials it.*) One pound eight and four, then. It's been awfully nice chatting with you, Miss Moon.
(HORNIMAN *enters.*)

ANN: I've enjoyed it, too, but I hope you won't be dead before evening. Population explosion or no population explosion, it's rather interesting to be somebody. Considering the alternative, it's fascinating. And I know *I* wouldn't care to be dead suddenly. Not for all the money in the world. Me for me and my poverty for ever.

SAM: Life is surely more than just selfishness.

ANN: How much more? Forget it. For all we know, tomorrow money may be abolished by law.

SAM: Are you a Communist of some kind, or what, Miss Moon?

21

ANN: Oh no, I'm studying ballet. To me everything's a dance. Always has been. Do you dance?

SAM: No, but I'd like to learn. I mean, I wish we could talk some more sometime. Could we?

ANN: I don't know why not.

SAM: I'm at Number Thirty-three East Best-Two-Out-of-Three. Where are you?

ANN: Angel Lane. Two twenty-two.

SAM: We're neighbours. Strange I've never seen you before.

ANN: I'm in town a lot.

SAM: May I call?

ANN: Of course. May I?

SAM: May you? I should say you may. We're not rich yet, of course.

ANN: You don't have to be rich.

SAM: Don't you?

ANN: Of course not. Good-bye. Take care. Don't be a fool if you can possibly manage.

SAM: Really? Why?

ANN: Well, I suppose it's because I like you.

SAM: You don't!

ANN: I do. And I'd like to see you again. Why wouldn't I?

SAM: Well, I never imagined a girl who is studying ballet would like me.

ANN: And I won't forget the tuppence that came out of your own pocket.

SAM: Oh, it was nothing.

(ANN MOON *goes almost dancing.* SAM *smiles watching her go.* A GYPSY WOMAN *and a* TIPSTER *arrive outside the bank.*)

TIPSTER: All right, then. What are *you* selling?

GYPSY: For a shilling I'll read your palm. (TIPSTER *hands her shilling and holds out his hand.*) You have some connection with horses. Ninety-nine per cent you're a crook, one per cent doubtful, but your personality's good.

(*She goes to* SAM'S *window and reaches for the money.* HORNIMAN *stands near.*)

SAM: Oh no, madam, you're not allowed to *take* the money.

GYPSY: It's not yours.

(*She goes to* TED'S *window.*)

GYPSY: (*Places coins on counter.*) Give me silver for these coppers, boy. And for a shilling I'll read your palm.

TED: (*Gives her coin. Softly.*) For sixpence I'll read yours.

(*She holds out her hand.*)

I see a dark man in your life, and a lot of dirt on your hand.

GYPSY: Ah, you're a gypsy yourself, boy. I have a daughter who'll teach you the truth. She's eleven. Can you wait a year?

HORNIMAN: Conclude your transaction, Mr. Owlett. Conclude it.

(GYPSY *walks straight at* HORNIMAN *making him step out of her way.*)

(*The* TIPSTER *stops two men with newspapers.*)

TIPSTER: It would be a lie for any man in the world to pretend that he knows the winner of *any* horse race, but it is *not* a lie when I tell you that I know, because that is the truth. I *do* know. I'm not asking ten bob for this information, I'm not asking five bob. Half a crown is the price I ask, but try to get a secret from America for less than half a *million* pounds. I have the winner of the three-thirty at Alexander Park. Half a crown and he's yours.

(*The two men collect the tips, going around in circles, repeating the names after the* TIPSTER, *in confusion.*)

TIPSTER: Ike. Mac. Nik. Moa. Mike. Jack. Dick. Joe.

MAN: But which horse is going to win?

TIPSTER: That's all, boys. (*They freeze.*)

HORNIMAN: That was about the foolishness and desperation of

23

people wanting to get something for nothing. On another level, it was about other people and other things. Ike, Mac, Nik, Moa, Mike, Jack, Dick, Joe. These are the first names of an assortment of men who are presently world famous. Their last names aren't mentioned because in fifty years they may be forgotten, and then of course the names will stand for horses only. Which may be just as well, most likely.

(TIPSTER *enters bank*.)

TIPSTER: Let me have a quid for these coins, boy.

SAM: Yes sir. (TIPSTER *takes a wad of notes from his pocket*. SAM *seeing this*.) Wouldn't you like to open an account, sir?

TIPSTER: What for?

SAM: Money earns money, sir.

TIPSTER: How much money earns how much money?

SAM: Any amount earns two per cent per year.

TIPSTER: (*Handing him the wad*.) Two hundred and ninety-nine quid.

SAM: (*Finding one more*.) Three hundred. Your name, sir?

TIPSTER: My real name?

SAM: I'm afraid so.

TIPSTER: Tully Turnpenny.

SAM: Three hundred pounds, now on deposit and drawing two per cent interest per year in favour of Mr. Tully Turnpenny. Your address, sir?

TIPSTER: Five two seven Wapping Basin. Now, if you want to pick up a little easy money for yourself, my boy, back Dancing Girl in the four o'clock at Alexander Park. No charge.

SAM: Thank you, sir. (TIPSTER *goes*.)

(MR. HORNIMAN *watches* SAM *and nods with approval as* TED *notices*.)

HORNIMAN: Sam, in all the years of my banking experience, I have never seen a more brilliant beginning.

TED: He's as good as President of the bank already, and

24

I'm still nowhere, forty years later. (*Calls out to the two horse-players*.) Over here please, over here. Make your deposits over here, please.

HORNIMAN: Mr. Owlett. In a bank it is not proper to cry out like a street hawker.

TED: Sorry, sir.

HORNIMAN: Sorry's not enough. It may very well be that your place is not here face to face with the public. If so, I have other work for you.

TED: (*Quickly, fearfully*) Yes, sir, it may very well be, but I most certainly would appreciate another chance, sir.

HORNIMAN: You've already been at that window six years, but still hardly anybody favours you with a deposit. A few withdrawals every day, a few requests for loans without security, a few gypsies, and that's all. Are you sure banking is the career for you?

TED: Oh yes, sir, I live and breathe banking.

HORNIMAN: But almost nobody *proper* ever comes to your window, and when somebody proper finally does, your transaction is made in what appears to be bitter silence.

TED: Money is a strange thing, sir. It does strange things to people, sir.

HORNIMAN: (*Annoyed*) I beg your pardon, Mr. Owlett?

TED: I mean, sir, money seems to mean so much, sir, so *very* much to the people who come to my window, sir, that I hesitate to engage them in any kind of light talk, sir, but it isn't that I couldn't, sir, it's simply that I feel, sir, they would rather I didn't, sir.

HORNIMAN: It doesn't matter what you *imagine* they'd rather. It's part of your work to keep our transactions cheerful, hopeful, hearty, human, as Sam Hark-Harkalark does.

TED: Yes, sir. May I please have another chance, sir?

HORNIMAN: One more chance, then, Mr. Owlett, but that's all I can spare, I'm afraid. There is other work, The

25

wages are less, but the work may suit you better. You may be happier.

TED: Yes, sir, but I've never been happier than I am here.

HORNIMAN: Your happiness is so near despair, I wonder what your unhappiness is like.

TED: Cheerful, sir, hopeful, hearty, human, sir.

HORNIMAN: Try again, then. I shall be near observing.

TED: (*He gets to his knees.*) Yes, sir, thank you, sir.

HORNIMAN: All right now, I know I'm much too kind for my own good, but there is a limit, Mr. Owlett. Back to your place. *Attract* your transactions, as Mr. Hark-Harkalark does. I will not allow barking.

TED: No barking, sir. Thank you, sir. (HORNIMAN *goes.*) Dirty rat.

SAM: What's the matter, Ted?

TED: You're *doing* me, Sam. When did I ever do you? You're taking all the transactions. He wants to put me back to office boy. My wife'll kill me. My son'll hate me. My daughter'll laugh at me.

SAM: You're not married, Ted.

TED: I mean later. Send some of the transactions over here, will you?

SAM: How? I can't disappear, can I?

TED: Then, tell me what to do. What do you do?

SAM: I don't do anything. Stop worrying, will you? There's no need to worry.

TED: Oh no, no need at all. After six years at this window he wants to put me back to office boy, but there's no need to worry. I may have to pack up and go to Hong Kong or Singapore. New York or Hollywood. Far, far away. No need to worry at all, Sam.

SAM: Do you want me to tell Horniman I want to go back to office boy?

TED: He wouldn't think of letting *you* go back to office boy. Six years of fear and trembling for nothing.

SAM: What are you afraid of?

TED: Horniman. People. Cats. Dogs. Robbers. Gold fish.

Mistakes. Accidents. The H Bomb. I'm afraid of
everything. But now, since this morning, most of
all, I'm afraid of you, Sam. You're going to kill
me, I believe.

SAM: I'll go and tell him right now. I don't want the
promotion.

TED: Go and tell him *that*, and he won't put me back to
office boy, he'll *sack* me, that's what he'll do. Just
send some of the transactions over here.

SAM: Well, I'll do my best.

(WALLY WAILER, *a rock and roll singer, enters. He
plays guitar and sings. During song* PEARL GALWAY
*and an American soldier come on and dance, then go
their separate ways.*)

TED: Wally Wailer, the richest poor boy in London.

WALLY: We were only having fun,
You and I, Nellie Miller,
Arocking and arolling through the night,
When he came on the run, on the run, Nellie
Miller,
Flashed a knife and challenged me to fight.

Now, how was I to know you were his wife?
And how was I to know he was a killer?

I am sorry in the uproar,
I ran out of the nearest door,
But I had to, darling Nellie, for my life.

The tears are in my eyes, for all the world to see.
I am sorry you were killed, darling Nellie.
It was fate, I guess, or something just as bad.
I am sorry, but I'm glad it wasn't me.
Yes, I'm sorry, but I'm glad it wasn't me.
(SAM *hides under desk.*)

TED: I'll be happy to look after you, Mr. Wailer.

WALLY: No hurry. I'll wait. I'm superstitious. Move from
this window, and I might lose me voice.

27

TED: No, man, your voice is here to stay. Step right over.

WALLY: No thanks, I'll wait.

TED: (*To* SAM) Better come up, Sam. It's no use.

SAM: (*Comes up.*) Well, now, let's see what we have here. Two thousand pounds. Congratulations, Mr. Wailer, that's quite a sum.

WALLY: I feel most fortunate to have been given my glorious voice, and most grateful for the support of the public, and the devotion of the teenagers.

TED: *Ice* agers. *Stone* agers.

SAM: There it is, then, Mr. Wailer. You've got close to thirty thousand pounds in that account now, sir.

WALLY: But I really don't *care* for money, you understand. I'm paid in another coin. The affection of the people. The respect of the government. The love of the little children.

TED: How about cats? How are you doing with them?

SAM: England is proud of you.

WALLY: I am starting the Wally Wailer Foundation to encourage other young men of England to sing, as soon as I have fifty thousand pounds.

SAM: You're very kind.

WALLY: I couldn't succeed if I weren't.

SAM: You have set a noble example. (*Enter* DAISY DIMPLE.)

WALLY: I have tried. (*Going*) It isn't easy.

TED: Daisy Dimple herself. The most famous stripper in London, and of course she'll be coming straight to you, Sam.
(DAISY DIMPLE *goes straight to* SAM *and places a bank-book and some currency in front of him.*)

SAM: Would you mind very much stepping over to the other window, Miss Dimple?

DAISY: Why? What's wrong with this one?

SAM: Well, nothing really, but I thought you might not mind.

DAISY: Oh, I get it. You want to have a look at my back.

28

(*She shows her back.*)

SAM: Well, thank you, but I thought you might not mind letting my friend attend to your transaction.

DAISY: You mean, *you* don't want to see me?

SAM: Oh no, I'm delighted to see you.

TED: Go ahead, Sam, it's no use. I'll go to Tanganyika.

SAM: (*Counts* DAISY'S *money quickly and writes in book.*) Two hundred and ninety-three pounds. Thank you very much, Miss Dimple.

DAISY: (*Going*) See me at the Gargoyle, boys, the Keyhole, and the Nell Gwynne.
(*As she goes a young man walks across stage and notices* DAISY.)

TED: What foundation is *she* founding?
(*A* BLIND MAN *enters.*)

SAM: This one's for you, Ted. He's blind. Just hum something, I'll keep quiet, and he'll come to your window.

TED: "*Throw out the life line, throw out the life line—Somebody's going astray.*
Throw out the life line, throw out the life line—Somebody's drifting away."
(BLIND MAN *walks past* TED *to* SAM. SAM *doesn't move.*)

BLIND MAN: Well, come on, boy, let's deposit the money, shall we?

SAM: Why, yes, of course, but how did you know I was here? You can't see, can you?

BLIND MAN: No, but I know where to go. I can be walking slowly down Piccadilly with thousands of people moving towards me from front and back and I can always tell when somebody's going to drop a coin in the tin cup.

SAM: How?

BLIND MAN: Well, there's no how to it. I just know, and sure enough I soon hear the clink in the cup, and he's gone, whoever he was. If I don't get the feeling, I don't get the coin.

29

SAM: What's that got to do with coming to this window?
BLIND MAN: Well, not long ago you gave somebody a coin or two, didn't you?
SAM: Well, come to think of it, I did, at that. Ann Moon, tuppence.
BLIND MAN: Well, I knew that from ten feet off. So I came here. It isn't that anybody cheats a blind man. You might even put it the other way around, the blind man cheats others. It's just that I prefer to go to a giver instead of a taker, even though I myself am pretty much only a taker. I give a lot of people in the streets a moment or two of bad banjo music, and one or two of the people give me a coin. After four or five hours, it mounts up. After four or five years, it's quite a sum in the bank.
SAM: Sixteen thousand two hundred and eleven pounds, Mr. Gattling.
BLIND MAN: Thank you, my boy. I live well, and I like music. Not the music I make, you understand. I mean proper music. At home I listen only to the great ones. Haydn, Handel, Mozart. (*As he goes a girl walks across stage. Softer.*) Duke Ellington, Dizzy Gillespie, Harry Truman.
(INSPECTOR OVERBOARD *of Scotland Yard and an Interpol Observer from Russia*, CAPTAIN DATCHIKVILI, *enter outside the bank*.)
OVERBOARD: Now, here is a bank in a working-class neighbourhood of London where you might very well *expect* a hold-up now and then, or an *attempted* one, and yet the astonishing fact is that in the twenty-two years that I have been with Scotland Yard this bank has not been held-up.
DATCH.: There is always a first time, Inspector Overboard, and it will happen sooner or later. It *must* happen.
OVER.: Oh, I know how you feel about us, Captain Datchikvili, or how you believe you must feel in order to be a patriotic Russian, but now that you are an Interpol Observer in London, won't you

DATCH.: please forget it?
DATCH.: I will try, but this bank is *now* ready to be robbed.
OVER.: You're not trying, Captain Datchikvili.
DATCH.: As long as there is one empty stomach in this world I cannot permit myself to enjoy funny stories.
OVER.: I beg your pardon?
DATCH.: I am crazy about funny stories. Sometimes I can't control myself and I roar with laughter. And then I am ashamed for a long time. What right have I got to laugh as long as there is one empty stomach in this world?
OVER.: Well, can't you laugh and at the same time try to do something to fill the empty stomach?
DATCH.: No, that is not the way. You have your Christian sins and we have our Communist sins, and our biggest sin is to forget even for a moment the empty stomachs.
OVER.: Where are they? For the most part?
DATCH.: Where *aren't* they? They are everywhere. Right here. All over London. All over England. All over America, even.
OVER.: All over Russia?
DATCH.: Only between meals. Russian stomachs between meals become not empty but ready for more food. In the last five years the production of wheat, barley, oats, rye, beef, lamb, dairy products, eggs, cheese, butter, leaf and root vegetables, tea, tobacco, wine, vodka, brandy . . . the production of all these good things has increased thirty per cent.
OVER.: Well, I'm glad. Russia is a big country and her people are a fine people. I've seen your chaps on the football field and they're awfully good players.
DATCH.: In *all* things we are the best. Sports, theatre, ballet, music, science, rockets, medicine, machinery, electrical power, chess, diplomacy, education, and jonoujouk.

31

OVER.: What's that?

DATCH.: That is the little bone in the knee of the lamb, which the boys of Georgia, my own country, take out at the dinner table, clean and polish, and use in a tossing game which we call jonoujouk. We are the greatest at jonoujouk. Also the other things.

OVER.: Yes. Now, is there anything about this bank you would like to study in particular? Would you like to go in and meet the President?

DATCH.: No, it's a capitalist bank and it will soon be robbed. That is enough for me.

OVER.: A very poor man once went into a bank in London and asked to see the President.

DATCH.: Is this a funny story?

OVER.: Well, I don't know. When he saw the President he said, "Please forgive me for taking up your time, but I have never seen a million pounds and before I die, I want to do that."

DATCH.: Oh no, please stop. It's only the beginning and already I am laughing inside. No, no, I do not want to hear this story. A very poor man, that's the important thing. And it is not something to laugh at.

OVER.: The President of the bank happened to have in his vault at that time not one million pounds but ten million, and he invited the poor man to go into the vault with him to see the money. While they were in the vault the bank was held-up. A very alert young clerk quickly shut the vault door and turned the dial, so that the door could not be opened again for a week. The robbers went off with a comparatively small sum of money, and were later apprehended. In the meantime, the President of the bank informed the poor man that they could not expect to be released for a week.

DATCH.: *This* is a funny story?

OVER.: Perhaps not. At any rate, the poor man decided to count the money to pass the time, and so he had something to do. The President on the other hand could only think of his home and his wife and his children and his fire and his supper and his brandy after supper and his bed, and so he suffered terribly. At last, a week went by, and the door of the vault was opened.

DATCH.: Yes, yes, please don't stop.

OVER.: Now, in the meantime, all of London had taken a great deal of interest in their terrible ordeal. Which of them would die, which go mad, and so on.

DATCH.: Yes, yes.

OVER.: Well, they *both* marched out. The President of the bank went back to his work, and the poor man went back to the street.

DATCH.: I don't get it.

OVER.: I haven't finished.

DATCH.: All right, finish. I'm not laughing and I'm dying.

OVER.: The President turned out to be the poor man, and so of course the man who had gone out into the streets was actually the President. He was never seen again.

DATCH.: Either I am controlling myself very good, or this funny story is not funny.

OVER.: The point is that the same shocking experience can affect people differently.

DATCH.: The funny stories of Russia are *funny*.

OVER.: (*Going*) Ah, well. Perhaps it's just as well you didn't laugh, because it would only have made you feel guilty and unhappy. Shall we go along then?

BLIND MAN: (*To the audience.*) Now, you see, we've got all this stuff going on, all these people messing about the bank, and Stratford, and London, and of course we want to make something of it, but so far we haven't, have we? Well, it takes time.
(*Girl walks on stage carrying a revolver on a tray. He takes it.*)
This is a gun, a toy for idiots. The way it works is this. Gunpowder is made to explode, sending a

C   33

piece of metal somewhere, making the most useless
sound in the whole vocabulary of sounds. From
this beginning has come the machine-gun, the
cannon, the rocket, all of the bombs, and a million
variations of the one basic nothing sound. Bang!
Ridiculous, meaningless (*Enter* MAN *and* WOMAN),
a belittlement of silence, sound, and everything
worthwhile it has taken us centuries to make. This
noise, this insult to the human spirit, is heard in
many plays, so let's hear it too.

MAN-TO-BE-EXECUTED: (*After taking long puff at cigarette.*) My
name is—I can't remember my name. But I *am*
guilty—of trying to improve the world. *And*
myself—aren't you?
Long live the revolution.
Long live the counter-revolution.
Long live space.
Long live time.
Long live the truth.
Long live the lies.
Long live the cat.
Long live the mice.
And I'll never forgive you for this dirty crime.
(*He places blindfold over his eyes. Gun shot.* MAN
falls. Scream. Police whistle.)

WOMAN: Oh, my God.
(*Fish, dog, and teddy bear fall from above.* MAN
picks them up, hands one to WOMAN, *and they go off.*)

BLIND MAN: Nobody can say what just happened, because too
much happened at the same time, on account of the
inferior order of excitement created by the pistol
shot. And yet history is an elaborate and
inaccurate account of just such stuff, multiplied and
enlarged a million times. Thus, history is not
gospel, it is gossip. The gun then: noise, violence,
fear, hysteria, pain, confusion, grief, shame,
lies, death, and the fantasy memoirs of generals.
And that's enough of that.

34

(*Girl enters with tray and egg-beater. He puts the gun back and lifts the egg-beater.*)
What's this for?

GIRL: He didn't say. (*He looks at the egg-beater and puts it back. She goes.*)

BLIND MAN: Who *are* these people actually in the play so far?

SAM: On my word, I don't know, and for that matter I don't know who Sam is. Hark-Harkalark, that is. Myself. The character I'm playing. I don't understand the bloke.

BLIND MAN: You don't have to understand him. Just as nobody is required to understand himself. Just as nobody ever *has*, either. And that includes the greatest men you might care to bring to mind. You know their names. Great names. The greatest. If they *had* understood themselves, they might not have lived as they did, and we might not have had them brought to our attention so unforgettably. I am speaking very clearly and calmly because whenever somebody is saying very little or nothing at all, it is absolutely necessary that he be heard without excitement, otherwise it might be imagined that he *is* saying something, perhaps a great deal.
(*The* AMBASSADOR *comes down the aisle and up on to the stage.*)

SAM: (*To* AMBASSADOR) Yes sir, what is it?

AMBASSADOR: I am the Ambassador.

TED: For the love of God, great China hasn't been recognized by America yet—with more than six hundred million people. Don't tell me *we* have?

AMB.: I am the Ambassador from the *audience*. We want cordial relations with the play, and I have been sent to establish and maintain them.

SAM: Please do so, Mr. Ambassador.

AMB.: From the audience to the play, greetings. Sholem Aleichem.

SAM: Great writer. Great humorist.

AMB.: From the moment since the curtain went up we

35

have been here. And our seats are comfortable.

SAM: That's good.

AMB.: We are a civilized people.

SAM: That's good, too.

AMB.: And we hope that the play is also civilized. Is it?

SAM: Mr. Horniman, I think this question ought to be answered by you.

HORNIMAN: From the play to the audience, through its Ambassador. Our government rejoices in the friendship of your government, and prays for its continuance. For thirty-three minutes we have thrived upon the warmth of your proximity.

SAM: What's that mean?

HORNIMAN: Glad you're here. And we hope that you have found it possible to resist any impulse to abandon us.

SAM: What's that mean?

HORNIMAN: Don't go home.

SAM: Why should they? They've just come.

HORNIMAN: Diplomatic language. Although we are a new nation with an unrevealed identity, we live in the expectation of making our identity known, and having done so, we dare to hope that this revelation shall neither offend nor alarm you, but rather please and appeal to you.

SAM: What's that mean?

HORNIMAN: We like you, please like us.

SAM: That sounds like a square deal. What about the part about being civilized?

HORNIMAN: Well, of course, the answer is that we *are* civilized, because the audience is. In a sense you, the audience, are the play more than we are, for while we are the players who in concert are making the play, it is you, even more than we, who are the true players and the true play.

SAM: Are you *sure*?

HORNIMAN: No. We welcome your Ambassador, and look forward eagerly to a deepening.

SAM: Of what?

HORNIMAN: Everything, of course.

AMB.: Where do I sit?

SAM: A chair for the Ambassador, please.
(*A chair is brought out by the stage manager, and the* AMBASSADOR *sits down.*)

SAM: And now, Mr. Ambassador, how can we make you feel more at home? After all this must be a strange country for you.

AMB.: I would like to learn the language as quickly as possible. What is it?

SAM: Isn't it English?

AMB.: I do not mean the philologic language. What is the *inner* language of the play?

GYPSY: (*Who has just entered.*) Romany of course. Even all is not all. How could it ever be, since all has no beginning and no end?

SAM: What's that mean?

GYPSY: Live and let live. There is more to everything than anybody could ever guess. Nobody is greater than anybody else. Relax.

SAM: Did that help at all?

AMB.: Not really, but the fault may be mine. Now what's this play about?

SAM: The dead, the dying, and the unborn. In short, *us*.

AMB.: *All* of us?

SAM: We rather hope so.

AMB.: I see. Thank you.

SAM: On with the play then, please, everybody.
(*Off stage the cry of a London newsboy is heard.*)
"No war. How much longer can this go on? Too many people. Everybody wants to get into the act. World's number one problem is too many people. Too many people."

TED: Hear that, Sam? Too many people.

SAM: Yes, it's like I told Ann Moon. There's this population explosion.
(*Exit* HORNIMAN.)

37

TED: Ann Moon? Who's Ann Moon?

SAM: The girl who dances. You know. My second transaction. I'll never forget Ann Moon as long as I live.

TED: You gave her tuppence, didn't you?

SAM: I didn't mean to make it as public as all that.

TED: What'd you do it for? (AMBASSADOR *walks around them.*)

SAM: Oh, I don't know. It's not every day I get promoted. No, that's not what I mean. It's not every day I meet a girl like Ann Moon.

TED: Give every girl you meet tuppence, and you won't have very much left for yourself at the end of the week.

SAM: I enjoy giving. If I had a million pounds, I believe I'd give it away.

TED: It's easy to give away a million pounds when you haven't got it.

SAM: If *you* had a million pounds, would you give it away?

TED: Not tuppence. Why should I give away *my* million pounds?

SAM: You haven't got it. It doesn't cost anything to *want* to give it away.

TED: I don't want to.

SAM: I believe you *should* want to.

TED: I don't want to.

SAM: You'll never get rich.

TED: Did the rich get rich by giving away a million pounds?

SAM: I'm not talking about the rich. I'm talking about the poor with money.

TED: What poor with what money? If they've *got* money, they're not poor any more. They're rich, and how long does it take the poorest man in the world to know he's rich, and act accordingly?

SAM: How long?

TED: The transformation is instantaneous. No matter

38

what he was a moment ago, he becomes an instant blackguard. And wouldn't I like it to happen to me?

SAM: But you wouldn't give any of it to anybody else?

TED: I wouldn't.

SAM: Why not?

TED: I need all the help I can get from a million pounds.

SAM: Well, if you *had* a million, do you think *a million* would be enough?

TED: Yes, I believe it would.

SAM: You wouldn't be afraid any more?

TED: I wouldn't be afraid of Horniman any more. (*Quickly*) Here he comes. (TED *starts counting a bundle of notes quickly*)

HORNIMAN: (*With an armful of brand new notes*) Sam, as a reward for the brilliant beginning you have made on your very first day as a full-fledged clerk, I am bringing you *half a million pounds* in brand new five-pound notes.

SAM: Half a million, sir?

HORNIMAN: (*Proudly*) Half a million pounds.

SAM: Sir, isn't that just a little more than I am likely to need for the day's transactions?

HORNIMAN: Of course it is, and that's just the point. I know a banker when I see one. I want you to know my trust in you is absolute and implicit. That's what this means. Now, just sign this receipt, please. Count the money at your leisure. Always do that, Sam. Check the money. Make sure it's all there. If it isn't, say so. If there's more—well, I needn't urge you to report it. Right there.
(SAM, *with shaking hand, begins to sign.*)

SAM: I've run out of space here, sir.

HORNIMAN: Just turn the page over and spell out the rest of your name on the other side. (SAM *does so.*) Very good. (*He reads the signature.*) Sam Hark- (*Turns the slip of paper over.*) Harkalark. Carry on, then,

TED: Sir?

HORNIMAN: (*A little annoyed*) Yes, Mr. Owlett? What is it?

TED: Do you have any new notes for me, sir? To sign for?

HORNIMAN: Certainly not, Mr. Owlett. I will reward you when you deserve to be rewarded.

TED: Yes, sir. Thank you, sir.

HORNIMAN: Carry on.

TED: Sir?

HORNIMAN: (*Blowing up*) Yes? Please continue. Don't say sir, and stop.

TED: What can I *do* to deserve to be rewarded, sir?

HORNIMAN: Be a banker, Mr. Owlett. (*Emphatically*) Be a banker.

AMB.: Hold it. Hold it, please.

TED: Yes?

AMB.: What does the President of the bank mean by saying, "Be a banker, be a banker?"

TED: He means he wants me to stop being Edward Owlett, and I can't, because that's who I am, you see. Edward Owlett. Nobody else.

AMB.: Who would he prefer you to be?

TED: Well, nobody in particular. He just wants me to stop being me.

AMB.: Why?

TED: Well, you see, I've been at this bank so long and I've become so good at *seeming* to be awfully humble that he is beginning to suspect I consider bankers in general contemptible, and he himself the most contemptible banker of all.

AMB.: But he's not quite sure?

TED: Not quite. How could he be? With all my grovelling?

AMB.: The grovelling, then, is actually a performance?

TED: Yes, it is. Or at any rate, it began by being a performance six years ago, but little by little more than half of the time I forget that it *is* a performance and so it's real, too.

AMB.: Hadn't you better think of another career?

40

TED: I barely thought of this one.

AMB.: I think I understand now. I'm sorry I had to interrupt.

HORNIMAN: Not at all. We want you to interrupt whenever you feel the need of a certain amount of clarification.

AMB.: Is there anything *you* would care to add to Mr. Owlett's comments?

HORNIMAN: Sam, perhaps it would be more to the point if you added a word or two to Mr. Owlett's comments.

SAM: Ted's my best friend and he's got a great sense of humour. You never know when he's playing a practical joke and when he's serious. You might get the impression he hasn't got anything to live for, but I've seen Ted eat fish and chips and nobody who eats fish and chips the way Ted eats is entirely out of touch with the old human tradition of great expectations. Ted still expects plenty.

HORNIMAN: Thank you, Sam. I believe that threw a *little* additional light on the matter.
(Music like thunder is heard.)

SAM: (*To* AMBASSADOR) Now, that storm. Perhaps I'd better explain it. We just do that.

AMB.: You just *do* it? It doesn't mean anything?

SAM: What could it possibly mean? It's a storm. If we were not in London, if we were in another time entirely, an earlier time, the time of caves, for instance, it would mean we'd better get to the caves as quickly as possible.

AMB.: On account of the rain.

SAM: On account of our *fear*. Of the unknown. Of large things not understood. A kind of language unknown to us. A language of the gods, so to say. Or the language of God, the one God.

AMB.: I had no idea. Would it be asking too much to hear it again?

SAM: Do you really want to?

AMB.: Yes, I believe I do.

SAM: Again, please.

41

(*After listening, the* AMBASSADOR *blows his nose loudly.*)

SAM: Are you all right, Mr. Ambassador?

AMB.: Yes, yes, thank you, quite all right. It's just that for a moment there a strange feeling of loneliness took possession of me, and it rather hurt, I must say. Was that intended?

SAM: Well, no, but of course we're glad to accept just about anything of that order that might come along.

AMB.: And so there you are, the two of you, at work in the bank, one favoured, and one not. Now, what's going to happen?

SAM: Well, next is the hold-up.

AMB.: (*As* FATHER FINNEGAN *and the* GYPSY WOMAN *come in.*) The bank is to be robbed, is it?

FINNEGAN: (*As he speaks the* GYPSY WOMAN *draws near and looks intently at his face.*) In a manner of speaking, only. I am called Father Finnegan. Once a day I visit a bank somewhere in London. On my way to the bank, I pray. I ask for a small miracle. Nothing so extraordinary as the raising of the dead. I pray for money, on behalf of those who have not yet been born. Perhaps the miracle shall be a rich man near the end of his time, who shall in a sudden burst of understanding hand me a great sum of money. Or a thief who shall take it by force, and, while making his escape, hand it to me. I don't know *how* it shall happen, but here I am again, in another bank, in another neighbourhood of London, a total stranger. I have no business in *any* bank, but in my religion the bank is the church, and I come to it as others go to their Church. To me the shabbiest bank is even more beautiful than the greatest cathedral. For this is where the money is, and money is the true way, if only we knew.

AMB.: All the same, *you* shall rob this bank, is that it?

FINNEGAN: I don't believe so.

42

GYPSY: (*Points at* FATHER FINNEGAN.) That man lives by the grand and secret law which is beyond written law, and by which the Romany people have always lived in freedom—and poverty. He is out of Gemini.

FINNEGAN: Sagittarius, I believe, the Archer.

GYPSY: You were only *told* it was Sagittarius. You did not mark the time of your arrival, or the circumstance. It was marked for you, and inaccurately, as most markings are. Your mother perished, and your father was not there, knew nothing of you, lived and died knowing nothing of you.

FINNEGAN: You know me, Madam?

GYPSY: I do *now*. I didn't until I saw you, and I didn't see you until now. The concern of your whole life has been for the unwanted, the forsaken, the alone. Every dog has his day. Here is yours.

FINNEGAN: I stand here for a moment, is that right?

SAM: Yes, that's right.

HORNIMAN: Be a banker, Mr. Owlett, be a banker.

TED: Yes, sir.

HORNIMAN: Observe Mr. Hark-Harkalark, and learn how to be a banker.

TED: Yes, sir.

(HORNIMAN *goes.* TED *studies* FATHER FINNEGAN. *Begins to write a hold-up note, as a practical joke.* SAM *is busy counting the new bank-notes very quickly.* TED *observes him.*)
Oh, Sam's the banker, all right. You're the banker, aren't you, Sam?
(SAM *gestures that he's counting and isn't to be interrupted.* TED *holds the note before him, reads it.*)
"Put all of the money into the Qantas satchel or expect the worst. A word to the wise is sufficient. Q."

HORNIMAN: (*Quickly*) Will you come to my office a moment, please, Mr. Owlett?
(SAM *drops some notes, which scatter, and he stoops*

43

to pick them up. TED *places the hold-up note on*
SAM'S *counter.*)

FINNEGAN: Now?

GYPSY: Now.

(FINNEGAN *goes to* SAM'S *window.* SAM *gathers up the*
fallen notes, and stands. He finds FINNEGAN *at his*
window. He finds the hold-up note. He looks from
the note to FINNEGAN, *who now places the Qantas*
bag on the counter.)

SAM: (*Picks up the note, reads it very slowly.*) "Put all of
the money into the Qantas satchel or expect the
worst. A word to the wise is sufficient. Q." (*Aside*)
He can't do this. I'll press the button and sound
the alarm.

(*A large* WOMAN, *and a* MAN, *not together, come in.*
The MAN *carries a ticking clock.*)
Who are these people? Are they part of his gang?
What's that clock?

(*The* WOMAN *fishes through a small purse. The*
MAN *places the clock on the floor and searches*
through his pockets.)
Is it a bomb?

ANN: (*Comes in dancing.*) I'm coming to visit tonight at
seven. All right? (*She goes.*)

SAM: But I may not be able to make it tonight. I may be
dead. (*Suddenly*) *Dead?*
(*He begins to put the brand-new notes into the*
satchel.)

GYPSY: Oh, the purity of it, the absolute innocence, the
rightness, the beauty.

(FINNEGAN *looks up in gratitude, takes the satchel,*
bows to SAM, *and goes, slowly, to his table, and*
starts handing money to CORAL *and* PEARL.)

AMB.: Is *that* the robbery?

SAM: The first part of it.

AMB.: And who has seen it?

SAM: Well, I have and you have.

AMB.: And these other people?

44

SAM: They haven't. They've been busy with their own lives.

AMB.: Quite. (*Girls and* FINNEGAN *go.*)

TED: (*Returns*) Mr. Horniman has just been informed by the Bank of England that each of the new notes is defective and must be returned and destroyed.

SAM: What's the matter with them?

TED: G. O. Dodd, the Chief Cashier, who signs every Bank of England note . . . . well, it's too complicated to explain. The notes are signed Good God. Mr. Horniman wants me to take them back.

SAM: Well, it's too late, I'm afraid.

TED: Why?

SAM: The bank's been robbed.

TED: Well, press the alarm button, for God's sake. (SAM *presses the button. Swan Lake is heard. The* AMBASSADOR *gets to his feet, confused. The* MAN *and* WOMAN *imitate ballet dancers. The music stops.*)

SAM: The alarm has been sounded, and the robber can't be far, so I cry out: (*He speaks evenly.*) Stop that man. This cry is always for somebody harmless. Stop that man, he's taken my hat, for instance. It is never for anybody really sinister. Now, immediately after crying stop that man, I make a great leap over the counter. (*He takes one step.*) And then I run with all my might after the robber. (*He takes two steps.*) But this woman stands in my way. Not me, madam. And this man also stands in my way. Not me, sir. I'm Sam Hark-Harkalark. Well, all they know is that somebody cried stop that man, and I'm the only man who's moving, so of course they believe I must be the man to stop. But I break through just in time to come face to face with a London Bobby who wants to catch the bank robber. There I stand like Oliver Twist scrubbed and bathed, and here comes the club. (*The Bobby strikes him over the head.*) Now, here, we could have had a song and dance, if we really

45

wanted to:

> If the bloke who spoke out of turn,
> And was hit over the head, isn't down or dead,
> Hit him another over the head.
> Hit him another over the head.

(*The Bobby hits him another over the head.*)
Now, I'm out like a light. Cold. Cancelled.
Changed. (*He makes a stiff fall and is caught by
the* MAN *with the clock, who lets him down gently,
flat on his back.*) Second part of the robbery.

HORNIMAN: (*Enters.*) Is that Sam? (TED *nods. He goes to* SAM.)
What's the matter with Sam?

CLOCK: He robbed the bank, but we caught him, didn't
we?

WOMAN: I'd very much like to faint, if I may.

CLOCK: By all means. (*She leans back. He supports her.*)

HORNIMAN: *Sam* robbed the bank? Mr. Owlett, do you know
anything about this?

TED: No, sir. I was in your office at the time.

HORNIMAN: Are you *sure* you know nothing about this?

TED: Only what Sam told me when I came back to
fetch the defective notes. They were gone.

HORNIMAN: All of them?

TED: Yes, sir.

HORNIMAN: (*Looking up. His mind working quickly.*) All *two
million pounds*, Mr. Owlett?

TED: Two million, sir? Wasn't it half a million?

HORNIMAN: *Two million*, Mr. Owlett. They were all gone?

TED: (*Catching on*) Yes, sir.

HORNIMAN: Well, wake him up. We've got to ask him to
identify the robber.

CLOCK: You mean, *he* isn't the robber?

HORNIMAN: I'm not sure. In any case, I'm very sorry, but this
is the end of the banking career of Sam
Hark-Harkalark. Bring him along to my office
then, please, officer.
(*They all go off leaving* TED *to look after the two
transactions. The* WOMAN *changes twelve pennies*

46

for a shilling and departs. MAN *with clock goes to* TED'S *window, presents his book, and some money for deposit.*)

TED: (*Aside*) Be a banker, be a banker. (*Marks book.*) Thank you, Mr. Wiseguy.

CLOCK: Who?

TED: (*Looks at name in book again.*) Wiseguy? Isn't that what it says here? Artie Wiseguy?

CLOCK: Well, *you* wrote it. I opened this account with you five years ago. Can't you read your own handwriting?

TED: I'm sorry, sir. I must have written Wiseguy. Isn't that your name?

CLOCK: My name is Arthur Wishingwell.

TED: Artie Wiseguy is the name that's in the book, sir.

CLOCK: I don't care what name is in the book, it's not my name.

TED: Well, you've always got your address. Three thirty-nine Cobbler's Road.

CLOCK: Is that written in there, too?

TED: Yes, of course. Isn't three thirty-nine Cobbler's Road your address?

CLOCK: No, it's *not* my address.

TED: That's what's in the book.

CLOCK: Well, is the book *my* book?

TED: It's the book you *brought*.

CLOCK: How much is in the account?

TED: A hundred and thirty-seven pounds seven shillings and thruppence. Is that correct?

CLOCK: No, it's *not* correct.

TED: How much do you make it?

CLOCK: *One thousand,* one hundred and thirty-seven pounds, seven shillings and thruppence.

TED: Somebody left off a one up at the top of the figures, I expect.

CLOCK: Let me look at that book.

TED: Yes, sir. (*He hands him the book.*)

CLOCK: The name written here is quite clearly Arthur

47

Wishingwell. *My* name. The address is five twenty-five Upper Crown Road, and that's my address. The amount in the account is *one thousand* one hundred and thirty-seven pounds seven shillings and thruppence. All very clearly written.

TED: Then, everything's all right?

CLOCK: Well, I don't know. *Now*. How do I draw out my money?

TED: Well, you just take your book to the bank and say so.

CLOCK: Well, here's my book and I'm saying so. I want to draw out all of my money.

TED: Yes, that's exactly the way to do it, and then the clerk will count out the money and give it to you, minus a closing charge of tuppence.

CLOCK: Well, *you're* the clerk. Take your tuppence and give me the rest. If this is banking, I'd rather put my money in a cracked teapot.

TED: Yes, sir, but of course accidents *will* happen and people *will* make mistakes.

CLOCK: Not at a bank, on *my* money, they won't.

TED: Sometimes the mistakes are in *your favour*, sir.

CLOCK: Well, here's another pound. Deposit it.

TED: (*Takes the pound note and enters it in the book.*) Thank you, sir.

CLOCK: (*Looks into book.*) Well, this time you *haven't* made a mistake.

TED: I'm sorry. Better luck next time, perhaps.

CLOCK: Now, if you *had* made a mistake, if you had written *two* thousand one hundred and thirty-eight pounds seven shillings and thruppence, instead of one thousand, and I asked you to close the account, would you hand me two thousand one hundred and thirty-eight pounds seven shillings and thruppence?

TED: Oh yes, sir, minus of course the closing charge of tuppence. Is that what I wrote? *Two* thousand?

CLOCK: No, it's still one thousand.

(OVERBOARD, DATCHIKVILI *and a* DOCTOR *walk across the stage*.)

OVER.: By jove, you were right about the robbery. Two million pounds.

TED: *Half* a million.

OVER.: A gang, most likely.
(*They go into* HORNIMAN'S *office*.)

CLOCK: (*Gets out another pound. Places it on the counter with his book*.)

TED: What's this?

CLOCK: I'd like to deposit another pound.

TED: (*Makes the entry in the book*.) Yes, sir. Thank you, sir. (*They both sing* TEA FOR TWO. CLOCK *takes the book*.) Any mistake?

CLOCK: No, there isn't.

TED: Want to try again?

CLOCK: I don't know if I've got any more money on me. (*He searches his pockets*.)

TED: Smashing weather.

CLOCK: Yes, isn't it. No, I'm afraid I've deposited all the money I have.

TED: How about a game of tic-tac-toe?

CLOCK: Oh no, I've got to get back to work. I've got a dozen stopped clocks to fix, but I'll be back again soon, hoping for a favourable mistake.

TED: I'll be very careful. (CLOCK *salutes* TED, *who returns the salute, and* CLOCK *goes*.)

AMB.: You tried out a new way of being a banker, did you?

TED: Yes, and I must say, it worked very nicely, too. Now, Scotland Yard and Interpol are in Mr. Horniman's office asking Sam a lot of questions. And a Doctor.
(FATHER FINNEGAN *is seen seated at his desk miming distributing the money to imaginary girls*.)

TED: And that's Father Finnegan, handing out the money to the girls, of course.

AMB.: But where are the girls?

TED: They're right there, queued up.

AMB.: It isn't necessary for us to see them?

TED: *Five thousand* girls? Not until they make the movie.

(FATHER FINNEGAN *goes*. SAM *comes out of* HORNIMAN'S *office accompanied by the* DOCTOR, DATCHIKVILI, OVERBOARD, HORNIMAN *and a* POLICEMAN.)

DOCTOR: All right now, off we go to the clinic for x-rays. I'm afraid there *has* been a concussion, and you may have to go to hospital for observation.

SAM: You can go to hospital for observation. I'm going home. (*To* TED, *astonished*) He *sacked* me. He says I'm in on the robbery. He says I've been working a whole year with a gang of international crooks. He says there was no hold-up note.

TED: Well, he's wrong there. There *was* a hold-up note. I know there was.

HORNIMAN: How do you know, Mr. Owlett? You were in my office at the time of the robbery.

TED: Well, I know Sam wouldn't say there was a hold-up note if there wasn't one.

HORNIMAN: Well, where is it, then? We'll turn it over to Scotland Yard and in no time at all we'll know who wrote it, isn't that so, Inspector Overboard?

OVER.: Not quite. We'll know a little more than we know now.

SAM: He wants to put me in jail.

OVER.: There is no evidence at all that this lad is implicated in the robbery. The fact is, Mr. Horniman, I'm astonished that your own security officer was not on the premises.

HORNIMAN: As I told you, I was obliged to send him on a banking errand.

OVER.: And your alarm system works in a most peculiar manner, Mr. Horniman.

HORNIMAN: Well, a short circuit, most likely.

DOCTOR: Sam, how did you come by this name,

Hark-Harkalark?

SAM: My great-great-grandfather was stepped over in a pub by Shelley. Stepped right over him in the Green Man. Quite an honour. So he took the name.

DOCTOR: But I don't believe Shelley wrote that poem.

SAM: *Joe* Shelley? Of course he didn't. He didn't write *any* poem. He trained larks.

DOCTOR: Trained them to do what?

SAM: Not to *be* larks. Or at any rate to *try* not to be, high-larking about all the time, not a care in the world. Slowed them down. Taught them peace. Gave them dignity. A missionary he was.
(*The* DOCTOR *looks at* OVERBOARD, DATCHIKVILI, *and* HORNIMAN.)

TED: How's your head, Sam?

SAM: I don't know. (*Steps forward, smiles.*) Act One Finale now, complete with message: *People are O.K.*

BLIND MAN: The bank has been robbed. Who robbed the bank? Was it Father Finnegan, who went off with the money? (FINNEGAN *enters.*) Was it Ted Owlett who wrote the hold-up note, as a joke? Was it Sam, who put the money into the satchel? Was it Ann Moon, who planted the seed of fear in Sam's soul? (*Enter* ANN MOON.) Was it the alarm system which failed? Or did the human *conscience* rob the bank? (*Everybody comes on stage.*) It really doesn't matter, does it? The money is gone. There's plenty more where that came from. And where did it come from?

AMB.: It came from the people, of course.

POLICEMAN: Nothing is worth a damn without them.

DATCH.: Everything is *from* them and therefore must be *for* them.

GYPSY: They made religion, and they can throw it out, make it over, call it blasphemy, or let it please or bore them.

SAM: They made art, and they can take it or leave it,

51

believe or disbelieve it, use or refuse to use it.

TED: They made science. Science didn't make them. If science unmakes them, it won't be science, it will be a few of them unmaking the lot of them.

FINNEGAN: They very nearly made the universe by noticing it at all, making a guess and then a second guess.

OVER.: They invented the law, or no. And then they answered it with freedom, or yes.

ANN: In order to rejoice, they invented choice: yes or no, or yes for me and no for you.

HORNIMAN: Superior me, inferior you.

WALLY: They invented song and dance, wine, whisky, and games of chance.

TED: And then they did something very funny—they invented money.

BLIND MAN: If it weren't for the people the human race would fail.

TED: But who wants the human race? Its lazy, it's stupid, it hasn't got any class, it's crude.

HORNIMAN: It's always coughing, its nose is always running, and it always smells.

SAM: No government can afford to be rude, and so it will never be said to its face, but the fact of the matter is, to hell with the human race.

TED: Remember, it has not yet been established that the radioactive fall-out from H Bomb tests is destroying the human race at its source, in the genes. All we know at this point is that all over the world strange things are happening.

GALWAY: The radioactive fall-out isn't going to do anything strange to my baby, is it?

TED: Every government in the world is prepared to assure you again and again that nothing strange is going to happen to your baby—until it *does*.

HORNIMAN: May I remind you that the economy of the world is now sounder than it has ever before been, solely because of the enormous employment and business created by the rivalry between the great nations in connection with bombs, rockets, missiles, and other things of this sort which are still secret?

CLOCK: The making of destructive power?

HORNIMAN: Only *potentially* destructive. Only if *need* be.

SAM: And *he* sacked *me*. He said *I'm* part of an international gang of criminals. Oh, boy, get a load of him. (*To the audience*) And that's the end of Act One.

WALLY SINGS: Too many people, the wise men warn.
Too many kids who should never have been born.
Too many people who take too long to die.
Too many people, not counting you and I.

EVERYBODY: You and I are here to stay,
We are the wise men of the west.
Our fortunes grow from day to day,
And to hell with all the rest.

DANCING
AND
SINGING
Too many people, the wise men warn.
Too many kids who should never have been born.
Too many people who take too long to die.
Too many people, not counting you and I.

Act Two

At the bank, SAM'S *counter has been replaced by a small black tombstone:* SAM
> 1960

SAM *wears black athletic trunks, a white jersey with a large red number 1 on it, and white tennis shoes.*

By means of a plain chair, a pot-rack, and a long feather-duster, which he places on the floor, SAM *sets up the high-jump.*

SAM: Act Two. Now, this is where things get worse. Or better. Or stay the same. If we don't make it now, our goose is cooked.

AMB.: Now or never, is that it?

SAM: Precisely. What's the theatre for *now?* What can a play say that's *worth* saying now? Drop your bomb and be damned? Drop it or stop it? Were you proud to be a human being when we bombed Hiroshima? Around the moon the rockets fly, and here we are, not even flying a kite.

WALLY: *(Sings)* *Around the moon the rockets fly,*
Somebody help me fly this kite.
I only want to see the moon,
Flying in the night-time sky.
The day-time is the only time,
And darkness comes, too soon, too soon.
For me this world is quite all right,
Somebody help me fly this kite.

AMB.: What now?

SAM: We shall try to fly a *kite*, at any rate.

AMB.: Why?

SAM: This is not a Summit Meeting.

AMB.: Why not? I'm ready for a Summit Meeting if you are. I think we *ought* to discuss disarmament, nuclear tests, radioactive fall-out, and accidental war. Couldn't we have a touch of that in the play, too?

SAM: If you like.

AMB.: Stop wasting our money on weapons. Better schools and more teachers might be a good idea, for one thing. Stop polluting and poisoning the air of the world and the people who have to breathe the air. There must be better things to test, for better reasons. Stop making powerful weapons that any eccentric in a moment of emotionality might feel he must *use* in order to save civilization, or six or seven other things he might think of on the spur of the moment. In short, don't drop the bomb, boys. Your mothers will be ashamed of you.

SAM: That seems to cover the situation pretty well.

AMB.: I don't think the language was diplomatic enough, actually.

SAM: Meeting closed, and on with the play, Sam the Highest Jumper of Them All.
(*He turns quickly, to study the high-jump. The* AMBASSADOR *watches him a moment, and then stands to one side.*)

WALLY: (*Sings*)　*Who is old and who is new?*
Who can do what you can't do?
Sam—Sam, Hark-Harkalark.
Who knows all and more than all?
Who's got heart from wall to wall?
Who's the highest jumper of them all?
Sam's the man we're waiting for,
Nineteen years outside our door,
Except for Sam we'd be at war,
Sam the highest jumper of them all.

(*As* SAM *studies the high-jump,* ANN MOON *appears in his thinking, and then* TED, *and* MR. HORNIMAN. SAM'S GRANDMOTHER *stands near the tombstone, watching him. She carries his grey banking suit over her arm, and holds a sealed letter in her hand.*)

GRANDMA: Sam? (*There is no reaction from* SAM.) I could shout and I don't believe he'd hear me.
(SAM *moves slowly around the high-jump, followed by his* GRANDMOTHER, *whom he does not see.*)
(*The people who are in his thoughts speak softly.*)

ANN: Try not to be a fool, if you can manage. I'm coming to visit tonight at seven. All right?

TED: Oh, Sam's the banker all right. You're the banker, aren't you, Sam?

HORNIMAN: I am sorry, but this is the end of the banking career of Sam Hark-Harkalark.

GRANDMA: Sam! What's *this*, now?

SAM: (*Notices her for the first time.*) Oh, it's you, Gran.

GRANDMA: Well, who did you *think* it was?

SAM: Nobody, really. (*The three people go in silence.*)

GRANDMA: Now, Sam, they're coming at four, and you've simply got to be ready for them.

SAM: I wish you wouldn't interrupt me when I'm working.

GRANDMA: *Working*, Sam?

SAM: Yes, of course. I'm finding out what I've got to do next, and how I've got to do it.

GRANDMA: Well, just what do you *believe* you've got to do?

SAM: Jump.

GRANDMA: (*Indicates high-jump.*) Is that what that's for?

SAM: Yes, of course.

GRANDMA: And that get-up you've been in since morning?

SAM: These are my track clothes. You remember when I wore 'em at school.

GRANDMA: That was a long time ago, Sam, and you *were* at school, and that's all in the past.

SAM: Well, it's back in the present now.

GRANDMA: (*Pointedly*) Sam, the people who were here yesterday, and the day before, and the day before that, they're coming back again in a few minutes.

SAM: (*Indifferently*) Let 'em come. (*He begins to study the high-jump again.*)

GRANDMA: (*Quickly*) Don't you dare go back to work. I

tanned you when you were a small boy, when your
poor mother was killed in the blitz, and your poor
father was killed in Burma, fighting the heathen,
and you were fished out of the rubble and ruin of a
whole block of smashed houses, scratched and
bruised but still alive—I tanned you then, Sam, and
I'll do it again, if I must.

SAM: What heathen was he fighting?

GRANDMA: Oh, one of the various heathens. Now, you listen
to me. It isn't going to do for the visitors to see
you this way.

SAM: What way?

GRANDMA: First, you don't *look* right. Second, you don't
sound right. Third, you don't *act* right.

SAM: Who says so?

GRANDMA: They're beginning to say you're ill.

SAM: Crazy?

GRANDMA: They're *hinting* your grandfather and I must have
you looked after.

SAM: In the looney bin?

GRANDMA: For three hours last night your grandfather tried to
write a letter to *The Times*, another to the Home
Secretary, and another to a lawyer whose name he
got out of the telephone directory. But he *couldn't*
write to *them*, so he wrote to you, Sam.
(*She hands him the letter.*)

SAM: But I *see* him when he gets home from work.

GRANDMA: All the same, he wanted to write to you.
(*He opens the envelope, unfolds the sheet of paper,
turns it right side up, and reads the letter.*)

SAM: Sam, something's wrong somewhere, and it's not
your fault. But ever since the robbery, you're not
the same. If you can stop being changed, Sam, I
wish you would, because then I wouldn't need to
try to find out what's the matter. The trouble seems
small at first, but little by little it moves out until
it's the trouble with the whole world. And I'm too
old and ignorant to try to do anything about that,

57

Come back, if you can, Sam.

(SAM *thinks for a moment.*)

What does he mean?

GRANDMA: Stop being like this. *Think* before you speak. Help the police find the robber. Don't say the things you've been saying to the newspaper reporters.

SAM: What have I been saying?

GRANDMA: Don't you know?

SAM: They ask and I answer. Isn't that what I'm supposed to do?

GRANDMA: Your answers are too wise for a young man. It isn't wise to be wise, Sam. When you *are* wise, people have *got* to believe you're crazy.

SAM: Well, let's keep the reporters out of here, then.

GRANDMA: There's a bobby out front and another in the back to keep the reporters out, but some of the things you're saying are *still* getting in the papers.

SAM: Well, let's keep *everybody* out, then.

GRANDMA: You might as well know, Sam—*you're* being kept *in.*

SAM: I haven't wanted to go out.

GRANDMA: Yes, I know, but you're being kept in by the ones we *can't* keep out. Now, get into your grey banking suit, before they're here.

SAM: No, I'm going back to work the minute they're gone.

(*A door chime*)

GRANDMA: Well, it's too late now, I'm afraid. Please think before you speak.

(*She goes quickly.* SAM *watches her go, then shakes his head quickly several times as if to clear it. He steps back, and waits. The visitors are* INSPECTOR OVERBOARD, CAPTAIN DATCHIKVILI, *the* DOCTOR, *and a social-working* PRINCESS.)

OVER.: Well, how do you feel today, my boy?

SAM: Inspector, when you ask a question like that, do you expect the truth, or do you expect an answer that will please you?

OVER.: (*Looks at the* DOCTOR.) Well, you're quite right, Sam. I'm not a doctor, and so my question is academic. Let me put it this way. I hope you are well and happy.

SAM: I hope you are, too.

OVER.: Thank you. May I present her Serene Highness . . .

PRINCESS: No, no, please, Inspector. I am here *solely* as a social-worker. How do you do? (*She makes the royal wave of the arm twice, smiling with condescension.*)

SAM: How do you do?

PRINCESS: How many of you are there?

SAM: Just the one.

PRINCESS: Oh, no, I mean, how many in your family?

SAM: Three.

PRINCESS: You and your father and mother?

SAM: Grandfather and grandmother.

PRINCESS: And where are they?

SAM: (*Moves his head slightly.*) My grandmother let you in.

PRINCESS: And your grandfather—where is *he*?

SAM: I was about to tell you, but I needed just a little more time than you gave me. My grandfather's at work.

PRINCESS: What does he do?

SAM: He's a sandwich man.

PRINCESS: He makes sandwiches?

SAM: He wears them.

PRINCESS: He *wears* them? Is that possible?

SAM: Two sign boards.

PRINCESS: Oh yes, I believe I *did* see an old man doing that once: "Boycott South *American* Goods?" (*She means South African, of course.*) How long has he had the job?

SAM: Since yesterday morning. He had a lot of jobs like that until a year ago when I went to work at the bank and asked him to quit.

PRINCESS: You'd rather he didn't work?

59

SAM: Yes, of course.

PRINCESS: And your grandmother? Does she work?

SAM: She looks after my grandfather and me.

PRINCESS: Does that take up *all* of her time?

SAM: Yes, it does.

PRINCESS: (*With an unbelieving superior air*) Really?

GRANDMA: (*Annoyed*) Now, look here, Miss.

OVER.: Mrs. Hark-Harkalark! (*He goes to her and whispers.*)

GRANDMA: Yes, I *do* understand. And I would like to know how much longer my grandson and my husband and I must put up with this sort of thing?

PRINCESS: You know who I am, and you speak to me in that tone of voice?

GRANDMA: You are a social worker uninvited in this house, and I'm inviting you to get out.

PRINCESS: Doctor, have you questioned *her*?

DOCTOR: Yes, to a certain extent.

PRINCESS: And what have you learned?

DOCTOR: They're an old English family. Londoners.

PRINCESS: (*Glancing aloofly from one face to another, speaking in a witheringly soft and refined tone of voice.*) The situation is all too clear to me, and so I shall return immediately to the social centre and hand in my report.

DOCTOR: (*Holds out his arm.*) May I be permitted to urge you *not* to hand in a report at this time, please?

PRINCESS: You may not. (*She waves to the audience, and goes.*)

DOCTOR: Mrs. Hark-Harkalark, please don't worry about this, and may we be alone with Sam? (GRANDMA *goes.*) Sam, I notice a change in you. You're wearing tennis shoes and shorts and an athletic jersey with a large number one on it. Why?

SAM: (*Looks straight ahead, as if in a trance.*) Well, I just thought I wouldn't wear out my good clothes, so I put on these old clothes.

DOCTOR: And what's that over there? (*Indicates high-jump.*)

60

SAM: Oh, that's just a kind of haphazard arrangement of furniture.

DOCTOR: What's it for?

SAM: Nothing.

DOCTOR: It must be for something, Sam.

SAM: Well, maybe it's for looking at, then.

DOCTOR: But you're not looking at it.

SAM: Well, I thought my grandfather might enjoy looking at it when he came home from work.

DOCTOR: I'm sure he will. I know I enjoy looking at it. Does it have a purpose, Sam?

SAM: I don't know.

DOCTOR: Could it be something to jump over?

SAM: That's not for *you* to jump over, Doctor.

DOCTOR: Why not?

SAM: It's for *me* to jump over.

DOCTOR: Well, jump over it, then, Sam.

SAM: I'm not ready yet.

DOCTOR: You've got your tennis shoes on.

SAM: I've got to work before I jump.

DOCTOR: What sort of work?

SAM: I've got to think. I've got to learn a lot.

DOCTOR: About what?

SAM: About everything of course, because only by understanding a lot about everything will I be able to understand about jumping, too.

DOCTOR: What is it that you want to understand about jumping, Sam?

SAM: In the first place I want to find out what jumping is, and in the second place I want to find out how I am going to jump higher than any other human being has ever jumped.

DOCTOR: *You* want to jump higher than anybody else has ever jumped?

SAM: And I'm *going* to.

DOCTOR: Why?

SAM: I've *got* to.

DOCTOR: But *why*, Sam?

61

SAM: Why does anybody do anything harder or better than anybody else?

DOCTOR: Well, *you* tell *me*. Why?

SAM: To be somebody. That's why I'm going to jump very high.

DOCTOR: But that cross-bar can't be much more than two feet high. Anybody could jump over that.

SAM: I believe a good place to begin is at the beginning. A little while ago the cross-bar was on the floor.

DOCTOR: Did you jump over the bar, then?

SAM: No.

DOCTOR: Why not?

SAM: I'm studying the problem.

DOCTOR: When do you plan to jump?

SAM: When I'm sure I'll be able to jump higher than anybody else.

DOCTOR: I believe the world's record is higher than seven feet now, Sam. A chap in the United States.

SAM: Yes, I know. Seven feet, one and one-fifth inches, to be exact. John Thomas.

DOCTOR: (*Raising his arm.*) Seven feet *two* inches would be up about here, wouldn't it?

SAM: Yes, that's about right.

DOCTOR: That's pretty high, isn't it, for a chap your size?

SAM: Not if you understand everything the way I'm *beginning* to. I don't expect to jump until the cross-bar's at seven feet *three* inches.

DOCTOR: That's *awfully* high, Sam.

SAM: I may not jump until it's at seven feet four, or *five*, even.

DOCTOR: Why not?

SAM: Because I'll know I can do it, and the higher the better.

DOCTOR: For what?

SAM: For me. For jumping. For everybody. If I can do it, it can be done. And if it can be done in a simple thing like jumping, imagine the things that can be done in thinking.

62

DOCTOR: All right, Sam, let's say you've got the cross-bar at
seven feet five, and you're ready, and the whole
world's waiting to see you make the jump, how are
you going to do it?

SAM: Whoop, zoop, and over.

DOCTOR: Whoop, zoop, and over?

SAM: Whoop, zoop, and over.

DOCTOR: What's the whoop?

SAM: That's all your thinking, all your understanding,
all your concentration.

DOCTOR: And the zoop?

SAM: That's *demonstrating* it. Not an ounce of wasted
energy. Not a flicker of a flaw in the movement.
All of it pure, as natural and as easy as breathing
when you're asleep.

DOCTOR: Why not when you're awake?

SAM: Too many distractions. Too many things that have
no connection with the problem, but of course after
I've worked hard, even when I'm *awake* the
naturalness will be with me, and will carry me over.

DOCTOR: As light as a feather?

SAM: Nothing like that at all. A feather can only fall.
Only animals can jump.

DOCTOR: Birds *fly*.

SAM: That's another thing entirely.

DOCTOR: All right, then, let's say you *make* the jump, Sam.
What, then?

SAM: Everything.

DOCTOR: Well, specifically, what?

SAM: Fame, wealth, importance.

DOCTOR: You want to be rich and famous and important?

SAM: Who doesn't?

DOCTOR: Oh, I can imagine that a lot of people don't. I
might even say I don't.

SAM: Why not?

DOCTOR: I suppose it's because I know I *can't* be.

SAM: I don't know that. If I know anything, I know I
can be.

63

DOCTOR: By jumping?

SAM: As a beginning. One thing leads to another, you know.

DOCTOR: Sam, do you want my candid opinion?

SAM: I *know* your candid opinion.

DOCTOR: You can't do it, Sam. It's a physical impossibility.

SAM: Talk that way to Jesus walking water where would the world be?

DOCTOR: Then, being a good Christian is how you expect to do it, is that it?

SAM: No, because I'm not a Christian, good *or* bad.

DOCTOR: Why not?

SAM: Why should I spoil my average?

DOCTOR: What average is that?

SAM: My religion average. I'm none of any of 'em, but at the same time I'm a little of all of 'em.

DOCTOR: Are you a Jew, too?

SAM: Of course.

DOCTOR: And a Muslim?

SAM: Yes.

DOCTOR: A Buddhist?

SAM: Why not? A lot of people are Buddhists, and if there's something there for them, there must be a little something there for me, too.

DOCTOR: And races and colours, what about *them*, Sam?

SAM: I'm all races and colours, too.

DOCTOR: Are you a negro?

SAM: Of course. (*Remembering*) And there I stood all of a sudden—white! Drumming me toes on the Mission floor because all the others were black. Gad, what embarrassment, what inferiority.

DOCTOR: Sam, what do you believe in?

SAM: Freedom for India.

DOCTOR: But India *is* free.

SAM: I am speaking of *more* freedom. (*Pause*) For everybody. Everywhere.

DOCTOR: Freedom to do what?

SAM: To be alive decently, of course.

DOCTOR: All right, Sam. We'll talk again tomorrow.

SAM: You think I'm crazy, don't you?

DOCTOR: We don't use a word like crazy any more, Sam. It's really meaningless, you know. But I *do* believe something happened when you were hit over the head.

SAM: Bet your life something happened. I came to my senses.

DOCTOR: Well, let's hope so.

(DOCTOR, DATCHIKVILI *and* OVERBOARD *leave, and* SAM *goes off. The* BLIND MAN *enters.*)

BLIND MAN: Well, now, we've come to madness, haven't we? Our boy has flipped his lid. *Twice*. First when he put the money into the satchel, and then when he decided to jump higher than anybody else in the world. And so of course he *must* be mad. But he's fighting it out, as we all do. To be alive in the human body is the basic madness, which is common to all, since *this* animal would really prefer not to be an animal at all. But it's too late now, because long ago he exchanged his innocence, or ignorance, for wisdom, or guilt. Thus, sanity is simply the concealing of madness, and after centuries we have got pretty good at it.

(*Girl enters with the tray again. The* BLIND MAN *picks up the egg-beater. The girl goes. He holds it up.*)

This is an egg-beater, a toy for egg-eaters. The way it works is this. You turn this crank, and these blades go whirling around, making a sound that is not unpleasant to hear and can't hurt a fly. From this beginning has come the electrical mixer, in all of its various sizes and shapes, all drills, from the dentist's to the oceanographer's, the gramophone, the pencil-sharpener, automation in general, and the mechanical brain in particular. This brain is said to be capable of *thinking*, but so far the biggest one of all, at Harvard College (*Enter*

E

MAN-WHO-WAS-EXECUTED *and his wife*)
in the United States, a brain weighing ninety
thousand tons and occupying an area larger than
this theatre, has not even *accidentally* manufactured
one thought that might be considered real, unique,
original, or funny. Thus, the mechanical brain is
only an egg-beater in another form. The egg-beater
has been used only in those contemporary plays
which affected absolute realism and consequently
achieved a dull order of fantasy. Let us therefore
put the egg-beater to work in this play, too.
(MAN'S WIFE *is at* TED'S *counter in the bank .with a
bowl.* MAN *stands near by.*)

MAN: My name is John Edward George Henry London,
and I *am* guilty—of—being a willing slave. I work
all day, putting automobile motors together, one
little part into one larger part, which in turn is put
into a still larger part, until the whole automobile is
turned over to a cheerful idiot in a red jacket who
goes ninety miles an hour directly into a brick wall,
making a shambles of all my hard work. I come
home at night in despair, only to hear my cheerful
wife cheerfully whirling the egg-beater, making
another omelet, because I once made the mistake of
telling her she made the best omelets in the world,
and fifteen years and five kids later, she still wants
to bring romance back into our marriage. Well, it
can't be done, can it? But on she whirls and whirls,
ever hopeful.

MAN'S WIFE: Oh, hallo, dear. The omelet will be ready by
the time you take a shower, and change your
clothes.

MAN: Take a shower? Change my clothes?

WIFE: Yes, dear. And then I've made plans for the
evening.

MAN: You have? What sort of plans?

WIFE: Well. You know. A bottle of wine. Candlelight.
Soft music. Our song . . (*Sings opening two lines of*
66

Rule, Britannia!) You know.

MAN: Don't I, though?

WIFE: Do you like my dress? It's six years old, but I wear it only on special occasions, so it's as good as new. Do you like it?

MAN: Yeah, sure.

WIFE: And I've put six eggs in the omelet.

MAN: Six! What's that supposed to mean?

WIFE: Don't you remember?

MAN: Ah, yes. Who could forget?

(*Sings a little of* Rule, Britannia! *as he marches around the counter, puts his arms around her from the back, kisses her on the neck. She howls happily and whirls the egg-beater. He goes. She hands back the egg-beater, and goes.*)

BLIND MAN: It's fun. Being a survivor, I mean. It's *good* to be a survivor. But when I think of the millions who didn't make it, who were murdered, by *us*, I feel guilty all over again.

(TED *and* HORNIMAN *take their places.*) But that's another theme in another play, entirely. Back to this one, then.

TED: Sam's mad of course, and there's no telling *what's* going on in *his* head.

HORNIMAN: What are you mumbling about, Mr. Owlett?

TED: Sam, sir.

HORNIMAN: What about him?

TED: Sam's mad, but of course *we're* not, are we, Mr. Horniman?

HORNIMAN: You have not been at the bank thirty years. You are not permitted to address me as Mr. Horniman.

TED: Yes, sir. Why did you say two million pounds had been stolen when only half a million had, sir?

HORNIMAN: Two million pounds *were* stolen.

TED: Half a million by the robber, and a million and a half by *you*, sir?

HORNIMAN: That's right.

TED: What did you do it for, sir? It's against the law to

67

steal.

HORNIMAN: I know the law. I knew the law before you were born.

TED: What did you do it for, sir?

HORNIMAN: I might never again have such an excellent opportunity.

TED: Sir, how did you do it, exactly? I've given the matter a great deal of thought and I just can't understand how you did it, sir.

HORNIMAN: It was quite simple. The Bank of England sent me two million pounds. I delivered half a million to Sam, for which he signed a receipt. After the robbery, I changed the figures on the receipt from half a million to two million.

TED: *Forgery*, too, Mr. Horniman?

HORNIMAN: The *form*, Mr. Owlett! When will you understand the importance of the form.

TED: Forgery, too, *sir*?

HORNIMAN: No, not forgery at all. I simply *erased* the old figures and wrote in new ones.

TED: (*With feigned admiration*) And then, sir?

HORNIMAN: I took home the million and a half. They were defective in any case, as you know. Imagine the Chief Cashier G. O. Dodd, writing Good God instead.

TED: Yes, sir, I did imagine it.

HORNIMAN: Hence I have both the million and a half defective *plus* the two million covered by the insurance, *not* defective.

TED: Sir?

HORNIMAN: Yes, yes, I've told you a hundred times, don't say sir, and stop.

TED: Sir, now I'm *really* beginning to understand banking.

HORNIMAN: You're no good face to face with the public, and that's the first thing a banker's *got* to be.

TED: Sir, the public likes me.

HORNIMAN: They do?

TED: Yes, they do, sir.

HORNIMAN: Do they like me?

TED: No, they don't, sir.

HORNIMAN: Why not?

TED: There's something sneaky about you, sir. Crooked, clever, calculating, cagey, cruel.

HORNIMAN: Cruel, too?

TED: Sir, you are one of the cruellest nonentities of all time.

HORNIMAN: Well, it hasn't been easy.

TED: You'd cheat your mother, sir.

HORNIMAN: She cheated me.

TED: Sir, you'd open the tight little fists of ragged children in the streets and take sticky candy out of their hands.

HORNIMAN: Candy's not good for them.

TED: Sir, you'd leave the little children standing in the street with tears pouring out of their eyes.

HORNIMAN: Tears act as a cleansing agent and keep their eyes healthy.

TED: You are a criminal.

HORNIMAN: (*Blows up*) Mr. Owlett, unless you can respect the form of speech long established in this bank, I'm afraid I must put you back to office boy.

TED: Sir, I *can* respect the form of speech, and I *do* respect it, sir.

HORNIMAN: But you *forget* again and again.

TED: Sir, may I please have one more chance?

HORNIMAN: One more chance, then, but see that you don't forget again.

TED: (*On his knees*) Oh, I won't, sir. Thank you, sir.

HORNIMAN: (*Taking him by the elbow.*) All right, now. Up on your feet. (*He helps* TED *up.*) Back to work, then.

TED: Yes, sir. Thank you, sir.

HORNIMAN: Think about banking. Sam's all right. He's not crazy at all.

TED: Yes, sir. Banking. Not crazy at all, sir.

HORNIMAN: I know that foolish psychologist is trying to say

Sam's crazy, but *I say* the psychologist is crazy.
Sam's part of an international gang of crooks. We
have no evidence that he's *not*. Where's the hold-up
note, for instance? Sam will deliberately stay crazy
until he gets his cut of that stolen money.

TED: Yes, sir.

HORNIMAN: Did *you* see any hold-up note?

TED: *See* it sir?

HORNIMAN: No, of course not. *Nobody* saw it, because there
was none. It was Sam and his gang.

TED: Yes, sir, Sam and his gang, sir.

HORNIMAN: Do your work, then. (*He goes.*)

TED: I nearly lost my job again.
(*The* DOCTOR, *the* RUSSIAN *and* OVERBOARD *enter.*)

DOCTOR: Unless we can make Sam jump, I'm afraid he's in
serious trouble. Delusions of grandeur. Paranoia.
Schizophrenia.

OVER.: *Make* him jump?

DOCTOR: Oh no, we've got to encourage him to jump.

DATCH.: We do these things *also* much better in Russia.

DOCTOR: I've read accounts of some of your experiments,
and I must say they *are* impressive. Your method,
as I understand it, is love, home, and work. Well,
Sam *is* loved, and he *is* home, and so Sam *ought* to
go back to work, but of course Mr. Horniman
won't have him. If we can get Sam to jump, I'm
sure he'll be eager to seek employment at another
bank.

OVER.: The police are not finished with Sam yet, Doctor.

DOCTOR: Why not? That boy never stole anything in his life.
You know that, Inspector.

OVER.: I'm not saying he has, but it may very well be that
Sam is part of something he himself doesn't
understand. The fact is I'm baffled by the whole
thing. I have no reason to do so, but I feel that Mr.
Horniman is involved in the case in some way or
another, and of course *that's* ridiculous.

DATCH.: I don't like him.

70

OVER.: Why not?

DATCH.: I don't know. Now how do we get Sam to jump?

DOCTOR: Let me explain. And please do everything precisely as we plan. (*They go.*)

(FATHER FINNEGAN, *carrying the Qantas satchel, comes back into the bank. He goes to* TED'S *window, places a slip of paper on the counter.* TED *looks at him. Lifts the paper.*)

TED: (*Reading*) Put all of the money into the Qantas satchel or expect the worst. A word to the wise is sufficient. Q. (*Aside*) If Horniman finds me with this, he'll sack me. (*To* FINNEGAN) Did you write this?

FINNEGAN: Oh no. I found it at the bottom of the satchel, and I thought I'd better bring it back. Where's the other boy?

TED: Sam?

FINNEGAN: Well, I don't know his name.

TED: Sam Hark-Harkalark.

FINNEGAN: I believe that belongs to him.

TED: Well, he doesn't work here any more, but I'll give it to *him*. I know he'll thank you for it.

FINNEGAN: If you will tell me where I may find him, I would like to give it to him myself.

TED: (*Quickly*) Sam's in Patagonia. He lives there. All of Sam's people are Patagonians. Hark-Harkalark, that's an old Patagonian name.

FINNEGAN: But you said you'd give it to him.

TED: By post. I'd post it. Airmail. He'd get it in the morning. Don't worry about this little note, Sam'll get this note out there in Patagonia and be glad to have it back.

FINNEGAN: I wanted him to know how much good his kindness did in a frequently unkind and unfeeling world.

TED: I'll write it all down in my letter. How much good in a frequently unkind and unfeeling. They don't come like Sam any more. When they made Sam, they broke the mould.

FINNEGAN: And I wanted to shake his hand.

TED: (*Extends his hand.*) Yes, sir. I'll shake hands for Sam any day. (*He shakes hands vigorously, at the same time watching for* HORNIMAN.)

FINNEGAN: I'm flying home this afternoon after an absence of twenty-seven years, and I wanted to see one last time the only man I ever met who *understood*.

TED: Yes, sir, I don't understand the way Sam does, but I understand a little in my own way, and I'll put that in the letter, too. Back to Australia?

FINNEGAN: Oh no. I'm from Dublin. Well, actually a little out of Dublin. Killiney. I'll be there again long before the sun goes down.

TED: Yes, sir, back in Killiney before the sun goes down.

FINNEGAN: Tell him——(*He stops.*)

TED: Yes, sir?

FINNEGAN: I would like him to pick up where I leave off. To give as he has given, and to go on giving, even when he has nothing.

TED: Pick up, leave off. Give, go on giving, even nothing. I'll tell him.

FINNEGAN: Thank you.

TED: Glad to do it.

FINNEGAN: (*In the middle of the bank looking around.*) I want to remember this holy place.

TED: (*Nervously*) Yes, sir, holy.

FINNEGAN: Tell him . . . .

TED: (*One desperate wave*) I'll tell him *everything*. (FINNEGAN *goes as* HORNIMAN *arrives and watches him go.* TED *tries to make the hold-up note disappear but it remains in his hand.*)

HORNIMAN: Well, I see you've been at work for a change, Mr. Owlett.

TED: Yes, sir. I've been very busy face to face with the public.

HORNIMAN: What was that last transaction?

TED: Sir, that last transaction was a deposit.

HORNIMAN: Well, you see, when you put your mind to work, you *attract* deposits. You attract them, just as Sam——(*He stops suddenly.*) Well, there you are. (*He gazes down at the tombstone.*) Absolom, O Absolom. (*Angry*) Why do the most brilliant young men suddenly turn against their fathers, and join international gangs of thieves?

TED: Sir, maybe Sam *didn't* join an international gang of thieves. Maybe Sam ought to have his place back, sir.

HORNIMAN: (*Slowly, dramatically.*) Do you think I haven't wanted to ask him back a thousand times? I have. But no, no, not until he has confessed and paid his debt to society. Thirty or forty years at Wormwood Scrubs, but with good behaviour—(*Earnestly*) O Absolom, Absolom. Carry on. Attract another deposit. You're not Sam, but you're——

TED: Ted, sir. Teddy.

HORNIMAN: (*Annoyed*) Never mind that Teddy stuff, Mr. Owlett. You're a kind of rock. Simple and not very bright, but rocky. (*He looks at the tombstone again, shakes his head mournfully and goes.*)

TED: There must be an easier way to get rich. (*He puts the hold-up note in the inside pocket of his coat.*) (SAM *studies the cross-bar a moment, thinks deeply and suddenly makes a very good jump. He hears music from Capriccio Espagnol.* ANN MOON *comes running, kisses him, and runs off.* SAM *makes the jump again. The music again. Now,* DAISY DIMPLE, *in a razzle-dazzle costume, comes along.* SAM *takes one look, and extends an arm, stopping her.*)

DAISY: Don't you like me, Sam?

SAM: Of course I like you, Miss Dimple. But I don't want a Sex Bomb, who isn't anything else.

DAISY: But I'm not just a Sex Bomb, Sam. I'm an All-Around Bomb. A Cooking Bomb. A Sewing Bomb. I've got white teeth, and good strong bones,

73

SAM: You've got to be able to meet my intellectual friends, and they wouldn't expect you to dress like *that*.

DAISY: Don't you like the way I look?

SAM: I do, but what about my friends? And you've got to do something about your voice. All that low murmuring. They wouldn't understand you.

DAISY: But *you* understand me, don't you, Sam?

SAM: It's not enough for me to understand you. My friends have got to understand you, too.

DAISY: Oh no, Sam, let them understand somebody else.

SAM: I'm afraid it wouldn't work, Miss Dimple. I love Ann Moon, and we're going to be married.

DAISY: You could marry Ann Moon, and marry *me*, too, couldn't you? I mean, like on the side?

SAM: Oh no, I don't want to be a blackguard.

DAISY: It would be like you were two different Sams. One for her, and the blackguard for me.

SAM: But I *can't* be two different Sams.

DAISY: How do you know? Like have you tried?

SAM: Well, like I don't want to, because if I can be two, I can be three or four, too, and that's too many.

DAISY: Think it over, Sam. Like don't decide now. (*She goes, moving slowly.*)

(SAM *jumps again. Music. The* AMBASSADOR *stands.*)

AMB.: Sam. Now that you've jumped higher than anybody else in the world, tell me—how does it feel to be famous?

SAM: I was always famous. It's just that I never before did anything spectacular to demonstrate it.

AMB.: Then you don't really feel any different?

SAM: I don't think so.

AMB.: What about all the money you've earned? Has the money changed you?

SAM: No, I don't think so.

AMB.: But you *do* live in a mansion now, and you've got a summer home in Tanganyika.

SAM: Yes, I like to be where the lions are free. When

74

lions are out of cages, when they're home, they walk around as if the whole place had been made just for them. I like to see lions walking around that way.

AMB.: Suppose suddenly you lost your fortune, Sam? What would you do?

SAM: All of it?

AMB.: Every penny of it.

SAM: I'd go back to work.

AMB.: But you'd be awfully unhappy, wouldn't you?

SAM: I'd miss the lions a little.

AMB.: Not the money?

SAM: I'd miss the money, too, I suppose, but once you know you're poor again, you know, don't you?

AMB.: I hope you won't mind my saying so, Sam, but I expected you to be a little more—well, eccentric.

SAM: You mean crazy, don't you?

AMB.: Well, yes, on account of the distorted stories in the papers. Is that what happened?

SAM: I don't believe I've noticed what happened. What *did* happen?

AMB.: Well, first the robbery, of course. Then, at the same time, your decision to jump higher than anybody else in the world, but your refusal to jump *at all*. And then suddenly your jump of seven feet three and a half inches, followed by your tour around the world, jumping in every major city. Seven feet four inches in New York, four and a quarter in San Francisco, four and a half in Tokyo, five in Hong Kong, five and a half in Bombay, five and three-quarters in Athens, six in Rome, six and a half in Paris, seven in Berlin, seven feet seven and a quarter inches in Stockholm. All perfect jumps. And then in Moscow—total failure.

SAM: Total failure in Moscow?

AMB.: Well, I mean the first time. *You knocked down the cross-bar.* I think it's understandable we felt you'd been sabotaged. Especially after the Russians were

75

so tactless as to bring out their best jumpers, and Malko Duzka of Alma-Ata cleared the bar at seven feet seven and three-quarter inches, breaking your record by half an inch. How did that happen, Sam?

SAM: I told Malko how to do it.

AMB.: Why?

SAM: I told *all* of the jumpers how to do it. Malko understood best, I guess.

AMB.: What did you tell Malko?

SAM: Whoop, zoop and over. The Japanese insisted on translations and interpretations, and so did a lot of other people, but Malko didn't. He understood immediately.

AMB.: Weren't you annoyed when he broke your record?

SAM: No, I was glad. I hope he breaks it again.

AMB.: Not much chance of that, Sam. You went back to Karl Marx Stadium the following night in Moscow and cleared the bar at seven feet *nine* inches.

SAM: I wanted to give Malko and all the other jumpers of the future something to work for.

AMB.: At seven feet nine inches were you worried you might not be able to make it?

SAM: Yes, I was.

AMB.: You didn't want to let England down?

SAM: Well, yes, but it's not that alone. I didn't want this method of extending the human limits to fail, for any of us. And I was worried I might not be able to concentrate properly for seven feet nine inches, on account of the politics and propaganda that had come into the whole thing. Too many people were telling me I had to do it for England, and France, and Italy, and America, and the white race, and democracy, and freedom, and of course high jumping doesn't have anything to do with all those trade marks.

AMB.: Trade marks?

SAM: Yes, just like Bovril, Guinness, Schweppes, and all

76

the others.

AMB.: You couldn't concentrate?

SAM: Not the way I wanted to, because I began to *believe* in the trade marks. The people who wanted me to believe in them were such decent people, you know. They weren't fools. They were great men, some of them. And *they* believed in the trade marks, not blindly or unreasonably, but intelligently. They didn't *mean* to do it, but they made things awfully difficult for me in Moscow. It got so bad I began to believe I wouldn't be able to clear the bar at nine inches let alone *seven feet* nine inches.

AMB.: But you *did* clear it at seven feet nine inches.

SAM: Because before jumping I said that if I *did* clear it, it would be because I was jumping for people—for all people. And not for any government. And of course nobody was happier than Malko Duzka himself.

AMB.: Sam, may I ask a very difficult question?

SAM: Sure.

AMB.: What are we to do? All of us? All over. The world's smaller than ever and the weapons are greater than ever. Now, what are we to do?

SAM: We don't really have any choice, do we? We have got to put up with ourselves, haven't we?

AMB.: Yes, but how?

SAM: By not being afraid of one another, and by not scaring ourselves in trying to scare others.

AMB.: Individuals, or governments?

SAM: Both.

AMB.: One last question. Without war can the world economy be maintained? That is the question.

SAM: (*Jumps*) Yes.

AMB.: Thank you very much.

(SAM *goes off.*)

BLIND MAN: (*Enters*) Well, there's the theatre for you, and there's nothing like it. The last arena in which

77

everything is still possible. Well, Sam's winning his fight, as we have seen. He hasn't jumped higher than anybody else in the world, but he *has* jumped, and he may now be willing to believe that he *cannot* jump higher than anybody else in the world, or he may decide that he doesn't want to. We don't know, but we'll soon find out. (*He goes.*) (SAM, *dressed, comes in with a satchel. His* GRANDFATHER, *wearing a* News of the World *sign, comes in.*)

SAM: (*Quietly*) Are you finished for the day, Grandpa?

GRANDPA: No, I've got to go back for a couple more hours, but I want to be here when they arrive.

SAM: Let's not have any good-byes, shall we?

GRANDPA: You're not going anywhere, Sam.

SAM: I don't mind.

GRANDPA: I do.

SAM: If I'm crazy, I'm crazy. I didn't invent it.

GRANDPA: You're a great man.

SAM: No, I'm not.

GRANDPA: Well, if *you're* not, nobody is. Nobody ever has been.

SAM: A little maybe, *inside*. But I want to forget all about it, the same as everybody else.

GRANDPA: But you're not everybody else. You're Sam. No matter what happens, I want you to remember that. At first I wanted you to change back. To be the way you had been. But not any more. Whatever you do, don't change. Don't give over, like I did, like your father did, like everybody does. Giving over is even *worse* than being mad, Sam.
(*The* DOCTOR, OVERBOARD *and* DATCHIKVILI *are brought in by* SAM'S GRANDMOTHER. SAM'S GRANDFATHER *seizes* SAM'S *satchel.*)

DOCTOR: Not in your track clothes today, Sam?

GRANDPA: I don't want you to ask Sam any more questions, Doctor.

DOCTOR: I want to help Sam.

78

GRANDPA: I don't want you to help him.

DOCTOR: Sam's condition indicates the need of urgent therapeutic measures.

GRANDPA: I know all about Sam's condition. Unlike the rest of us, he's decently mad. We're just *sad* mad.

DOCTOR: I have had the authority for more than a week to take Sam away, but I have deliberately chosen not to exercise that authority.

GRANDPA: Don't speak that silly language of intimidation in this house, sir. I sat and talked with Sam until three this morning. Now, I'm going to ask you in a nice way to get out of here.

SAM: No, Grandpa, I don't want him to get out. Ask me any question you like, Doctor.

DOCTOR: I don't want to upset your grandfather, Sam.

SAM: Ask me anything.

DOCTOR: There's only one question *to* ask, Sam. (*Pause*) Do you still believe you can jump higher than anybody else in the world?

SAM: Yes, I do.

DOCTOR: (*Looks from one face to another.*) Well, I will go now, and I give you my word, sir, Sam will not be taken away from you until you *ask* that he be.

GRANDMA: Perhaps the doctor ought to be asked to stay with Sam a little longer.

GRANDPA: Do you want the doctor to stay?

GRANDMA: Yes, I do.

GRANDPA: Do you, Sam?

SAM: Yes, Grandpa.

GRANDPA: And if he believes you must be taken away?

SAM: How far away can anybody be taken? We're all here somewhere or other. Inspector, I don't know anything more about the robbery than I've already told you.

OVER.: I know that, Sam. We're at work on a number of other clues.

SAM: And, Doctor, I *am* mad.

GRANDMA: No, Sam, don't say that.

79

SAM: I *know* I am, Doctor, better than you could ever know or imagine, because it's *my* madness. And you can only know or imagine your own. What do you want to do?

DOCTOR: What do you want to do, Sam? Everybody here wants to help you. We even want to help you jump higher than anybody else. (SAM *turns*.) It isn't really impossible at all, Sam. When I said it was, I spoke foolishly. It *is* possible for you to jump seven feet, perhaps higher. And it may even be necessary for you to do so. If it is, we want to help you. But you must not jump now. Even *two* feet.

SAM: Why not?

DOCTOR: Oh, I know you *want* to, but don't do it, Sam. You're like a tiger who's got to leap across a great deep canyon. It's awfully far across. If you don't make it, you're gone. You've got to look across and keep looking.

SAM: (*Looks at the cross-bar.*) I'm looking now.

DOCTOR: And you want to jump, too. You think you're ready, but you're not. (SAM *stands, very relaxed. The* DOCTOR *looks at* OVERBOARD *and* DATCHIKVILI.) Hold him! Don't let him jump! (*They seize* SAM *suddenly, and they all fall.* SAM *gets up.*)

SAM: What's the matter with you blokes?

DOCTOR: Well, I guess our little scheme failed, Sam. You might as well know we tried to *trick* you into jumping.

SAM: You want me to jump?

DOCTOR: Yes, of course.

SAM: Why?

DOCTOR: Well, if you *would* jump, we'd know you're all right again.

SAM: (*Jumps quickly.*) Like this?

DOCTOR: How the devil did that happen? But you just said you still believe you can jump higher than anybody else in the world.

SAM: I still do, but I don't *want* to any more. On

80

account of my talk with my grandfather last night.

DOCTOR: Case closed. Patient restored.

(*To* GRANDFATHER) You have been most understanding, sir. I am a member of a profession it is impossible not to dislike now and then, but we have only three choices, God, family, or the psychiatrist. Last night you and Sam chose the family. It is a good choice.

(*He goes quickly.* OVERBOARD *and* DATCHIKVILI *nod and go.* SAM'S GRANDFATHER *goes.*)

SAM: (*Takes down the high jump.*) Well, we're almost home now, and so are you.

AMB.: Is this the end?

SAM: Well, actually, there *is* no end. There never is. We just like to start somewhere, and so of course we have *got* to stop somewhere. Anywhere will do.

AMB.: But so much is still unfinished.

SAM: Yes, that's how it always is. But soon morning comes, and we start all over again.

(*On the other side of the stage* TED *is at his counter.*)

(OVERBOARD *and* DATCHIKVILI *bring* HORNIMAN *out of his office.*)

TED: (*Astonished*) Sir?

HORNIMAN: I've told you a hundred times, don't say sir, and stop. What is it, Mr. Owlett?

TED: Why are the police holding your arms, sir?

HORNIMAN: That's precisely what I would like to know, Mr. Owlett.

OVER.: You're under arrest, Mr. Horniman.

TED: Oh, no, you can't arrest *him.* He's the President of the bank.

DATCH.: He is also a thief.

HORNIMAN: This is entirely the consequence of a misconception. No crime has been committed. A mistake has been made.

OVER.: Shall we go?

TED: Sir, they're taking you away.

HORNIMAN: Gentlemen, will you please be good enough to

listen to my faithful clerk.

OVER.: Have you something to say, Mr. Owlett?

HORNIMAN: Tell them, Mr. Owlett.

TED: Me? Tell them?

HORNIMAN: Yes, of course. My life's at stake. Tell them. (*He kneels.*) Ted. Teddy. Give me one more chance.

TED: This is entirely the consequence of a misconception. No crime has been committed. A mistake has been made.

HORNIMAN: (*Gets up.*) There, gentlemen. May I go, now?

OVER.: I'm afraid not. Actually, we solved the case soon after the robbery. It was simply a matter of getting the evidence, which we now have.

TED: Who robbed the bank?

OVER.: Mr. Horniman robbed the bank of a million and a half pounds. We found the money under his bed in a satchel.

HORNIMAN: It wasn't me.

TED: It wasn't him.

HORNIMAN: You will be promoted in the morning. It wasn't my bed.

TED: It wasn't his bed.

HORNIMAN: You will be Vice-President in the morning. It wasn't my satchel.

TED: It wasn't his satchel.

HORNIMAN: (*To* OVERBOARD, *annoyed*) I hope you're satisfied. All this humiliation in front of the whole world. There you are. The truth of the matter. My own clerk.

OVER.: Mr. Owlett will be expected to testify at the trial.

HORNIMAN: There must *be* no trial, gentlemen. We must think of the public, above all things.

OVER.: We *are* thinking of the public, Mr. Horniman. Come along.

HORNIMAN: One moment, please. Gentlemen, you are both men of the world. In the interest of the national economy, which will surely be undermined by a sensational trial, full of misunderstandings, distortions, clever legal questions, bewilderment, confusion, photographs, first person singular stories in the *Mirror*, *Sketch*, and *Graphic*: *don't do this thing*. You have a wife and three small children, I believe.

OVER.: And another coming.

HORNIMAN: I am prepared to undertake full responsibility for their well-being.

OVER.: So am I.

HORNIMAN: For every pound you are prepared to lavish upon these dear ones, the future statesmen, bankers, and captains of industry of proud England, I am prepared to lavish *two*.

OVER.: Shall we go?

HORNIMAN: Three, sir. (*To* DATCHIKVILI) And you, Captain, from beyond the iron curtain, in a free and prosperous world, *four*.

DATCH.: In Russia we would ask you four *thousand* funny questions.

OVER.: Come along, now.

HORNIMAN: Sound the alarm, Mr. Owlett. Can't you see the bank is being robbed.

TED: But the last time we sounded the alarm, it played *Swan Lake*.

HORNIMAN: I pray you, sir. Sound the alarm.
(TED *presses the alarm button. This time the music is from "Le Cid" by Massenet.*)

HORNIMAN: (*Loudly, over the music*) You see me here, ye Gods, one of the mighty falling, a poor old man, as full of grief as age, wretched in both. If it be you that turn these hearts against their father, fill me with noble anger. But soft! How sweet the moonlight sleeps upon this bank. What violent light out yonder circles and breaks amidst the galaxy? It is the East. The stars, the moon, the sun, undone. All undone.

SAM: End of Act Two, and end of the play, Sam the Highest Jumper of Them All, or the London

83

Comedy.

AMB.: What about Act Three?

SAM: That's outside, where we shall all soon be. Good-bye, then. God bless, good luck, until we meet again. (*He shakes hands with the* AMBASSADOR *who goes across the orchestra pit.*) On with the world, then. Thank you very much.

OVER.: Shall we go, then?

HORNIMAN: (*Being dragged away*) A misconception, gentlemen. A misconception.

(WALLY WAILER *plays and sings "We Were Only Having Fun", and the whole company sings and dances, as the curtain comes down.*)

(*The End*)

THE BALLAD OF NELLIE MILLER

Words and Music By William Saroyan

FIGHT ___ NOW HOW WAS I TO KNOW YOU WERE HIS WIFE ___

___ AND HOW WAS I TO KNOW HE WAS A KILLER ___

___ I AM SORRY IN THE UP—ROAR. I

RAN OUT THE NEAREST DOOR BUT I HAD TO DARLING

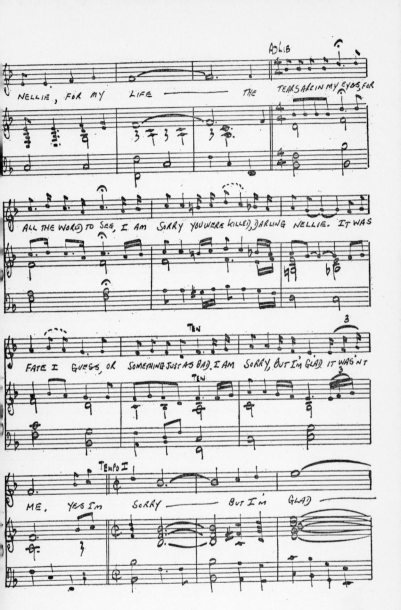

NELLIE, FOR MY LIFE — THE TEARS ARE IN MY EYES, FOR ALL THE WORLD TO SEE, I AM SORRY YOU WERE KILLED, DARLING NELLIE. IT WAS FATE I GUESS, OR SOMETHING JUST AS BAD, I AM SORRY, BUT I'M GLAD, IT WASN'T ME, YES I'M SORRY — BUT I'M GLAD —

IT WAS'NT ME

Too Many People

WORDS AND MUSIC BY WILLIAM SAROYAN

(SLOWLY)

TOO MANY PEOPLE, THE WISE MEN WARN, TO MANY KIDS, WHO SHOULD NEVER HAVE BEEN BORN. TOO MANY PEOPLE, WHO TAKE TOO LONG TO DIE ___ TOO MANY PEOPLE, NOT COUNTING YOU AND I

89

YOU AND I ARE HERE TO STAY_____ WE ARE THE WISE MEN OF THE

WEST___ OUR FORTUNES GROW FROM DAY TO DAY___ AND TO

HELL WITH ALL THE REST. (TEMPO) TOO MANY PEO-

-PLE THE WISE MEN WARN___

TOO MANY KIDS WHO SHOULD NEVER HAVE BEEN BORN.

TOO MANY PEO—PLE, WHO TAKE TOO LONG TO DIE

TOO MANY PEOPLE, NOT COUN-TING

YOU AND I

91

ME THIS WORLD IS QUITE ALLRIGHT, SOMEBODY HELP ME BEFORE I DIE.

SAM THE HIGHEST JUMPER OF THEM ALL

WORDS AND MUSIC BY WILLIAM SAROYAN.

WHO IS OLD AND WHO IS NEW WHO CAN DO WHAT YOU CAN'T DO SAM— SAM, HARK HARK A LARK—

WHO KNOWS ALL AND MORE THAN ALL, WHO'S GOT HEART FROM WALL TO WALL, WHO'S THE HIGHEST JUMPER OF THEM ALL SAMS THE MAN WE'RE WAITING FOR, NINETEEN YEARS OUTSIDE OUR DOOR, EX-

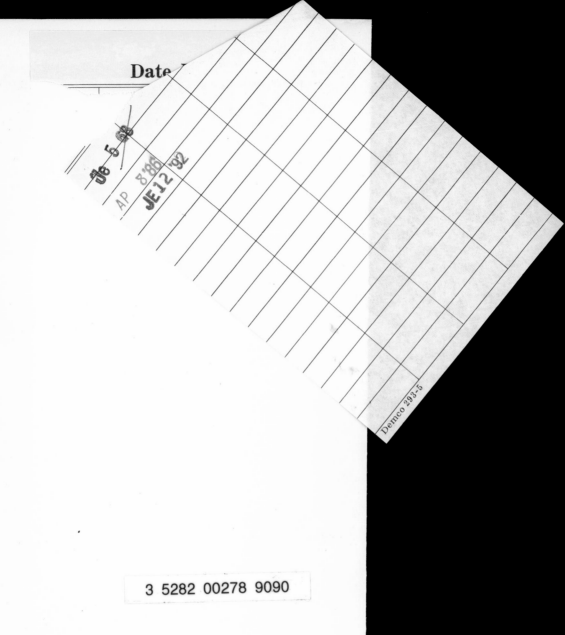